'Prisons are places that offer time to reflec
reveal. There can be tensions between loss
learn; grief and hope; resentment and reper
that transformation is possible. It is encouraging to read how we can
all turn our backs on the past and move forward with fresh hope.'
Michael Kavanagh – Chaplain General of Prisons

'We launched Prison HOPE, together with other leaders, in an
endeavour to support local churches in their work with people in the
criminal justice system. Through growing local links with prisons,
victim services and other organisations, churches can serve God,
helping some of the most vulnerable in our communities. These
stories from prisoners, chaplains and ex-prisoners give us all an
opportunity to appreciate more deeply the hope we can each discover
in the message of Christ.'
Rt Rev James Langstaff – Bishop of Rochester and Bishop to Prisons

'We are delighted to recommend *40 Stories of Hope* as the CTBI
Lent Course for 2018. The stories give a unique insight into prison
life and point to the hope we can find as followers of Jesus. The
group studies provide the whole Church – inside and outside prison
– with the opportunity to walk with Jesus through Lent, learning
from Mark's Gospel and from the lessons prisoners, ex-prisoners
and chaplains have learned. Whether we take this spiritual journey
through Lent, alone or in company, there is much to draw on to
refresh and encourage our faith.'
Bob Fyffe – General Secretary, Churches Together in Britain and Ireland

'Wherever we are, whoever we are, whatever we have done or failed
to do – the desire and need for hope unites us all. Each day I go into
different prisons across our country and each day I see the hope and
light of the gospel reaching into the lives of women and men, staff
and prisoners. The stories in this book are written so that wherever
you read them, whoever you read them with, you also have the
opportunity to glimpse the life-giving hope that Jesus Christ brings.'
Rev Helen Dearnley – Chaplaincy HQ Advisor, Her Majesty's Prison and
Probation Service

'The beauty of the Christian faith is that the unmerited grace of God is given freely to all who believe. As a result, men and women, no matter their personal circumstances, can have a personal relationship with God through his son Jesus Christ. These real-life stories show that beauty.'

Pastor Agu Irukwu – Jesus House, Redeemed Christian Church of God UK

'These 40 stories show that prisons can be a place of hope. As those in prison and outside prison read these wonderful stories and Mark's Gospel together, may we all experience a renewed revelation of Jesus, wherever we are.'

Rev Bob Wilson – Free Churches Faith Advisor to Prisons

'These inspiring stories show that prison walls are no barrier to the reach of Jesus, who longs to restore even the most damaged life. They challenge us all to walk with him more closely and proclaim him more confidently.'

Rev Phil Chadder – Chaplaincy Training and Development Officer, Her Majesty's Prison and Probation Service

40 STORIES OF HOPE

How faith has changed prisoners' lives

Compiled by Catherine Butcher

Foreword by Justin Welby
ARCHBISHOP OF CANTERBURY

HOPE brings UK churches together, using words and actions to see individuals and communities transformed by Jesus' love. Find out more at **www.hopetogether.org.uk**

© HOPE, 2017.

HOPE is a Registered Charity – Number 1116005.

Published 2017 by Waverley Abbey Resources, Waverley Abbey House, Waverley Lane, Farnham, Surrey GU9 8EP, UK.

Waverley Abbey Resources is a trading name of CWR. CWR is a Registered Charity – Number 294387 and a Limited Company registered in England – Registration Number 1990308.

Reprinted 2018, 2021.

For a list of National Distributors, visit waverleyabbeyresources.org/distributors

Scripture references are taken from the Holy Bible, New International Reader's Version® NIrV®. Copyright©1995, 1996, 1998, 2013 by Biblica, Inc.® Used by permission of Biblica, Inc.® All rights reserved worldwide.

Other versions used: Scripture marked ESV taken from the ESV® Bible (The Holy Bible, English Standard Version®), Copyright © 2001 by Crossway, a publishing ministry of Good News Publishers. Used by permission. All rights reserved.

Scripture marked NIV taken from The Holy Bible, New International Version®, NIV® copyright © 1973, 1978, 1984, 2011 by Biblica, Inc.© Used by permission. All rights reserved worldwide.

Scripture marked The Message. Copyright © 1993, 1994, 1995, 1996, 2000, 2001, 2002. Used by permission of NavPress Publishing Group.

Editing, design and production by Waverley Abbey Resources.

Every effort has been made to ensure that this book contains the correct permissions and references, but if anything has been inadvertently overlooked the Publisher will be pleased to make the necessary arrangements at the first opportunity. Please contact the Publisher directly.

Printed in the UK by Yeomans

ISBN: 978-1-78259-759-9

Contents

Foreword

This is an extraordinary book – a book of hope and reconciliation; a book of transformation and journeys. These 40 stories are a vital reminder of the hope that Jesus gives. They show us how lives can be transformed, and forgiveness can be found in the most unlikely places. There is no one, no life, no story that is beyond God's power to love and transform into renewal. Reconciliation is at the heart of it: reconciliation with ourselves in the face of shame and guilt about the past; reconciliation within families, friends and relationships; and most importantly, reconciliation with a loving God in the person of Jesus Christ.

Many of the prisoners who have shared their stories in this book have discovered life-changing truth. God hears us when we pray. He forgives us when we ask for his forgiveness, so that we can experience a profound sense of freedom – whether we are in a prison or a palace.

I am grateful to HOPE Together for bringing these stories together, and for their focus on linking churches and Christians outside and inside prison. This is a response to Jesus' call in Matthew 25 to be with those who are in prison. At the heart of the Christian gospel is the idea that everybody needs the presence of Jesus in their life. There isn't one of us for whom it doesn't matter. All of us have sinned and fallen short of the glory of God, as the apostle Paul says. And yet, there isn't one of us who is not loved and cherished by God. And God does not just want us to worship him, or go to church, or even have good lives. God wants a relationship with each and every one of us, whoever we are, wherever we have come from, and whatever we have done or left undone.

Like the prisoner who wrote: 'I used to think taking drugs was exciting, but now I wake up excited each day and talk with the creator of the universe', we can all discover this relationship. It is particularly wonderful to have these stories to read in the weeks before Easter. The resurrection of Christ is the hope for our world, because it proclaims the defeat of all that is evil and destroys human nature.

Whether you are reading this book alone or as a group, I pray that God may speak to you and equip you to bring hope to others as you draw on the faith, hope and love that only Jesus can give.

Justin Welby, Archbishop of Canterbury

Introduction

My first visit to a prison made a huge impact on me. I was struck by the number of young people – and the sad statistic that seven out of ten young people released from prison reoffend within one year. The charity I worked for then launched an initiative called Reflex to empower children, young people and young adults to break the cycle of offending and re-offending. I haven't stopped wanting to bring hope to people in prison.

When I met Lee, whose story begins on page 13, I was thrilled. Here was a man who'd been twice pardoned – once by an earthly king, and also by the King of kings – God himself. All of us have the opportunity to be forgiven. Because of Jesus, we can have the fresh start that we all need. Whatever our background, accepting Jesus' forgiveness means we can be adopted as sons and daughters of God. The 40 prisoners' stories in this book are an inspiration. But for the grace of God, any of us could have ended up behind bars. Because of Jesus' death and resurrection, we can all become part of God's family and live a new life.

HOW TO USE THIS BOOK

We have published *40 Days of Hope* to encourage you with the stories of how prisoners and ex-prisoners have found hope. This book can be used at any time, by individuals or groups, inside and outside prison. In 2018, it was used in prisons and in churches, particularly in the six weeks before Easter in 2018 – the season in the Christian calendar known as Lent.

Whenever you choose to use this book:

- Read the verses from the Bible, asking God to speak to you
- Talk to God using the prayers
- Consider how you can find fresh hope in your life
- Pass it on – how can you help others find hope?

We all face tough times and difficult challenges in life. We need hope. You might be reading this book alone in a prison cell, at home or with others in a group. Wherever you are, the HOPE Together team are praying that you will find hope for yourself in the stories you read over the next 40 days.

Each day there are Bible verses about Jesus to read and to think about. If you want to read the verses in the context of the whole of Jesus' story, you will find them in the Gospel of Mark.

Mark wrote his Gospel around AD 60 – only a few decades after Jesus rose from the dead. There were hundreds of eyewitnesses to Jesus' life who were still alive. You can trust that what Mark says about Jesus is true.

Mark's Gospel is part of the Bible. The Bible is an amazing collection of books written over about 1,500 years by 40 different authors. It is God's story, and shows how he is involved in human lives. God uses the Bible to speak to us today. Whether you have read the Bible before or not, ask God to help you to understand what he is saying to you. You could start each day with this simple prayer:

Dear God, please help me to understand what you are saying to me today through this Bible story. Please speak to me and help me to learn from you. Amen. ('Amen' means 'so be it'.)

Every day has an additional prayer for you to say, or you can use your own words to pray. You can talk to God out loud or silently. You don't need to use special language or a special voice. God knows us better than we know ourselves. Jesus said we can call God 'Father' or 'Daddy'. He wants us to be part of his family.

Alongside a Bible story, short thought and prayer, each day there is a story written by someone in prison or who has been in prison. Many have been supplied by prison chaplains. Most of the stories are anonymous, or names have been changed. Where the story has been published elsewhere, details are given so you can read more for yourself.

GROUP DISCUSSIONS

As well as the daily stories, prayers and Bible readings, there are six 'Looking back, looking forward' sections. If you are reading the book daily through Lent beginning on Ash Wednesday, these sections fall on Sundays, but they can be used on any day of the week. You can use these sections alone, or as part of a group (where, ideally, each member of the group will be using the book every day). When the group gets together you can discuss what you have learned. Let each person speak if they want to, and be sure to listen carefully to each person's contribution. Try to talk about your own life and the hope you are finding in what you are reading every day. Aim to make your group a safe place for people to be honest about themselves. Each person has a different story. Try to respect each other's views.

We trust that you will find fresh hope as you use this book over the next 40 days – and most of all, we pray that you will come closer to the source of all hope – Jesus, the central character in all the stories you will read.

Roy Crowne, on behalf of HOPE Together

A KING'S PARDON

Twenty years ago, I was living in Gibraltar. My mother had recently died and I was grieving. I am an only child and never knew my dad. I was approached to carry a suitcase from Thailand. Despite knowing that if I got caught I would probably be executed, I went, took the case, and was arrested at the airport. The authorities had been tipped off before I even got there. I was given a 'death sentence' which in Thailand equates to 200 years.

I had a five-kilo set of chains hammered to my ankles, had my hair and eyebrows shaved off, and was led off to spend the rest of my life in Bang Kwang maximum security prison. I shared a cell with 40 other chained prisoners for 18 hours a day, with one hole in the floor for a toilet. I was 27.

I made friends with a prisoner who had a missionary called Susan come to visit him. Whenever she had another person with her, she would try to get me called out of the cell too.

Unforgettable

After two years, the conditions got so unbearable, I opted for solitary confinement: locked up 24–7 in an eight by six foot cell infested with rats, mosquitos and cockroaches... but at least I was alone. It was in solitary that I started to read my Bible. One day, I got to the part where Jesus read Isaiah 61 in the synagogue (Luke 4:16–21). It stopped me in my tracks. Jesus proclaimed not only to heal the blind and the deaf, but also to free those that are captive and those that were bound. I will never forget my plea to Jesus that day.

My health started to deteriorate after three years. I had contracted tuberculosis and went from weighing 75 kilos to 45 kilos in a matter of weeks. The British Embassy kindly applied on my behalf to the prison authorities, asking if I could return to England once cured – not to change my Thai sentence, but so I could serve out its remainder in humane conditions. It was a long shot with a lengthy process, but I had nothing to lose.

Request granted

Five years later, after having served ten years, my request was granted. My chains were removed. I was flown back to England to HMP Wandsworth to await transfer to HMP Parkhurst on the Isle of Wight (due to my considerable sentence). However, the day before I was due to go, I was informed I would be going to HMP Rye Hill instead.

In Rye Hill chapel, after an event, I walked up to the piano and played something I vaguely remembered from piano lessons. I went back to my cell and thought no more of it, but about 20 minutes later I could hear cell observation flaps being slammed open and shut. The officers were looking for someone along the landing. The flap opened on my cell and an officer asked me if I was the guy that had been playing the piano. Was I really in so much trouble for that?

Chance meeting

The cell door opened and there was a short, blonde lady telling me she was a minister in the chapel. Could I come back and play something? I went back and played a few short pieces of classical music. She explained that they had been praying for a pianist. Would I like to come and play hymns for them? I remembered the prison I would still be in if it weren't for God. How could I possibly refuse?

I began working as a chapel orderly, building up a repertoire of over 200 hymns for services. Then, one day, a man called Paul came to give a Christian talk. I recognised him immediately. He had been to the prison in Thailand! What were the chances of meeting him here in England?

Paul said that, if I ever got released, I should look him up. In my mind I thought, 'That's never going to happen.' I had resigned myself to the fact that I would spend the rest of my life in prison – but I was forgetting, God always keeps his promises.

Royal pardon

One day, my cell door flew open. After having been in prison a total of 15 years, the officer informed me I had been given the Thai king's royal pardon and was to be released immediately! Thirty minutes later, I found myself on the other side of the gate with £40 in my pocket, and a feeling of complete and utter bewilderment. To tell you the truth, I didn't know whether to laugh or cry!

I spent the next two years working all over the country. I attained three forklift licences and bought myself a motorbike, but my company lost its contract. I had to find a new job. What was I going to do?

Then I got a call from Paul, asking me how things were going. I explained my situation and he suggested I use my forklift skills in Milton Keynes, where there were plenty of warehouses. So, that's what I did for the next two years. I bought a caravan to live in, but sometimes, as crazy as it sounds, I wished I was back in prison playing hymns in the chapel. Despite being free, I had no sense of purpose. I kept working, but I wasn't making any friends. I was living in fear, with feelings of shame. All I was doing was chasing wage packets from week to week, and I felt as if I had lost touch with God. But God had not lost touch with me.

New direction

I got a call from a guy called Steve I had met when he worked in HMP Rye Hill. He was a mutual friend of Paul's. I opened my heart and explained my situation. Steve told me that he now worked for a former chapel orderly called Simon. He had been released three years previously. He had been given a vision by God to start his own organisation in Stoke called Walk Ministries.

I had a number of conversations with Simon, the CEO, and he offered me a one-bedroom flat to stay in while I was with the project. There would be Bible studies, discipleship, counselling for post-traumatic stress, courses on personal development skills with modules on self-esteem, citizenship, social interaction, how to form lasting and meaningful relationships, and a 12-week leadership course. As well as that, they were looking for suitable trainees to work within the organisation. This was exactly what I had needed five years earlier!

Stable job

I worked for Walk Ministries for 14 months as Simon's personal assistant. When I moved on from Walk, I decided to stay in Stoke, where I felt accepted. I now have a forklift job with a permanent contract, and I am excited about the new opportunities that are ahead.

I believe I am exactly where God wants me to be: in the right place, at the right time, with the right people, doing what I believe is the right thing. I go to an amazing House of Prayer, and also to a local Methodist Church.

God's goodness and mercy follow us all the days of our lives. He always finishes the good work he has started in us, and he most certainly never gives up on us!

Contributed by Lee, an ex-offender.

01 There is hope

I didn't grow up wanting to commit a violent crime. In fact, the first crime I ever committed was to break into my primary school to set the hamsters free!

I grew up wanting to fit in, wanting to belong. But 'fitting in' on my street meant I was on amphetamines by the age of 15. Thirteen years later, on 15 September 1998, I decided I was done with life. I had no ambition and nothing to live for, and attempted to take my own life. I failed.

For a while after that, things started to look up. I moved away, got a job, met a girl and had three beautiful kids. But the drugs were always under the surface.

Emptiness

When we split up, I hit the drugs hard and I started drinking a lot. I was in 'our house' but I was alone. I thought drugs would fill the emptiness, but they lost me my house, my relationships and eventually my freedom. I ended up in situations I never would have dreamt of being in – at my worst, I got so high that I committed an offence that cost a man his life.

When there was a knock at the door, I knew it was the police. And when the charge came, I was relieved. It was like a weight lifted from me. I knew I'd done wrong and wanted to pay. And when the cell door closed behind me, the reality that I had taken part in a man's death hit me and I fell apart.

New life

I had nothing else left to lose, and so when the chaplain asked to pray for me, I said yes. As they did so, I felt something. I felt it again every time they prayed. I wanted to know what it was, so I started to go to chapel and attend their groups to find out more. The more I knew, the more weight was lifted off me. I knew I had done wrong, but now I knew that Jesus had paid for that. I didn't have it all figured out, but I knew I needed to give myself to Jesus. It felt like I had been stripped back to the bare minimum in order to be built back up to who I really was meant to be.

In November 2016, a few months after getting out, I decided I was truly done with my old life, and so I got baptised. I get to start life again – this time knowing that I belong, knowing I have family and knowing I don't have to do it alone. This time I know that when tough times come, Jesus walks with me. I know that I can handle it with his strength, and not mine. I know that I can run towards his open arms and not to the drugs. I don't have enough praise or thanks for what he has done. For the first time in 43 years, I feel alive and my smile is real. I thought I had lost everything, but I hadn't. Don't give up. There is hope. His name is Jesus.

Contributed by an ex-offender.

MARK 1:4,7-11

'John the Baptist appeared in the desert. He preached that people should be baptized and turn away from their sins. Then God would forgive them...

Here is what John was preaching. "After me, there is someone coming who is more powerful than I am. I'm not good enough to bend down and untie his sandals. I baptize you with water. But he will baptize you with the Holy Spirit."

At that time Jesus came from Nazareth in Galilee. John baptized Jesus in the Jordan River. Jesus was coming up out of the water. Just then he saw heaven being torn open. Jesus saw the Holy Spirit coming down on him like a dove. A voice spoke to him from heaven. It said, "You are my Son, and I love you. I am very pleased with you."'

SOMETHING TO THINK ABOUT

John the Baptist lived about 2,000 years ago in the Middle East. He challenged people to be baptised in water to show they were sorry for everything they had done wrong. He was preparing the way for Jesus, who takes our empty, broken lives and fills them with his new life. That's what John meant when he said, 'he will baptize you with the Holy Spirit'.

Jesus asked John to baptize him, even though Jesus had never done anything wrong. Jesus came to show people what God is like. His baptism was the start of this ministry.

God marked this special moment by identifying Jesus as his Son. And he said these remarkable words: 'I love you. I am very pleased with you.' At the time, Jesus had not done anything special. God's love for him was based on relationship. It's the same for us! God loves us and is pleased with us because of the relationship we have with his Son Jesus. There is hope! The stories in this book will help to explain what that means, over the next 40 days.

Prayer

Thank you, God, for loving me. I'm sorry for the wrong I do. Please change me from the inside. Amen.

'Here is what love is. It is not that we loved God. It is that he loved us and sent his Son to give his life to pay for our sins.'

1 JOHN 4:10

02 Good news

I don't know about you, but for me, the glass is always completely full. It's not half empty, and it's not even half full – it's completely full! And it's a good job that I never lost hope – because I have really made a mess of things in the past. I've had it all.

I've been an orphan; I've been a son (I was adopted at the age of three days, against my mother's wishes – or so I now know).

I grew up feeling rejected and abandoned; now, I've been accepted and found.

I've been married; I've been separated and divorced.

I've been loved; I've been hated.

I've been financially successful; I've been bankrupt.

I've lived in my own house, mortgage free; I've been homeless; I've lived in a caravan.

I've met the future king of England, Prince Charles; I've lived at Her Majesty's Pleasure.

I've owned top-of-the-range executive cars; I have lost everything and had my car towed away.

I've driven Lamborghinis; I've had to rely on my feet and public transport.

I've flown a plane; I've certainly been brought back down to earth with a bump.

I've travelled the world; I've been stuck in a rut.

I've partied and danced, celebrated and socialised; I've sat alone with no friends.

I've been a number; I've been a name.

I'm proud of some of my achievements; I am ashamed of so many of my mistakes.

But I am not my past. Spectacular sin and epic failures demand radical redemption, unfailing forgiveness and a deep-rooted rebirth.

They say people can't change – and I agree! People can't change, and certainly people can't change people, but God can! God can change people. Isn't that what the gospel is all about – what Christianity is all about – people who need to change their lives, coming to know Christ and seeing their lives changed!

For me, life changed when, in the deepest, darkest depths of my despair, all alone in my prison cell, I read the Bible from cover to cover... and it changed something in me. It changed *me*! I found hope – I found *the* hope! Christ alone can take your guilt and shame.

Roller-coaster ride!

When I left prison, some five or six years ago now, I knew the only thing I had to do was find a church. This, I did, but I found a whole lot more.

From three days old – feeling unloved and unwanted, rejected and abandoned – to where I am today has been an amazing journey. It's been the scariest and wildest roller-coaster ride that I've ever been on, with amazing highs to heart-wrenching lows... and it's not over yet.

God has also truly blessed me with my beautiful wife. She has shown me what it is to accept someone, unconditionally, just as they are – with all their hurts, habits and hang-ups – with all their flaws, faults and failures (and I still have many). I was a leper in society, longing to belong, and she came along with a whole lot of love.

I'm just an ordinary guy – you, too, can find hope, wherever you are.

Contributed by an ex-offender.

MARK 1:12-15

'At once the Holy Spirit sent Jesus out into the desert. He was in the desert 40 days. There Satan tempted him. The wild animals didn't harm Jesus. Angels took care of him. After John was put in prison, Jesus went into Galilee. He preached the good news of God. "The time has come," he said. "The kingdom of God has come near. Turn away from your sins and believe the good news!"'

SOMETHING TO THINK ABOUT

Jesus and John's lives went from the best of days to the worst. They had heard God speak as Jesus was baptised. But soon after, John ended up in prison. Jesus spent 40 days in the desert being tempted to deny God. Matthew, one of Jesus' close friends, wrote afterwards that Jesus had nothing to eat for those 40 days. Jesus used words from the Bible to beat Satan. (You can read more about this in Matthew 4.) We will all be tested, but we can be ready to respond the way Jesus did. Over the next few weeks, we will discover more about the 'good news' Jesus preached.

Prayer

Father in heaven, thank you for giving us the power to resist temptation. Please help me today. Amen.

'The LORD is tender and kind. He is gracious.
He is slow to get angry. He is full of love.
He won't keep bringing charges against us.
He won't stay angry with us forever.
He doesn't punish us for our sins as much as we should be punished.
He doesn't pay us back in keeping with the evil things we've done.
He loves those who have respect for him.
His love is as high as the heavens are above the earth.
He has removed our sins from us.
He has removed them as far as the east is from the west.'

PSALM 103:8-12

03 A new purpose

By the time she turned 27, Mary Kay had established herself as one of the most notorious criminals in the USA. Along with her husband, Mary Kay was wanted in four states for a string of bank robberies and was the target of a mafia 'hit' for double-crossing the mob on a diamond heist. She appeared on the FBI's '10 most wanted' list. It seemed likely that Mary Kay's life would come to a violent end.

But God had a different plan. In 1972, Mary Kay was arrested, convicted, and sentenced to 21 years in an Alabama prison. And it was in that prison that God called her to a new life. Flipping through a Bible one evening, Mary Kay read Ezekiel 36:26–27:

> 'I will give you new hearts. I will give you a new spirit that is faithful to me. I will remove your stubborn hearts from you. I will give you hearts that obey me. I will put my Spirit in you. I will make you want to obey my rules. I want you to be careful to keep my laws.'

'OK, God,' she prayed in her cell that night, 'if you will do that for me, I will give the rest of my life back to you.'

The result of that promise was Angel Tree, a Prison Fellowship programme designed to share God's love by helping to meet the physical, emotional, and spiritual needs of the families of prisoners. Since it began in 1982, Angel Tree has served over ten million children, providing them with Christmas gifts from their parents in prison, as well as mentoring opportunities. Families have been restored, and the good news of Jesus has been shared.

Families restored

After Mary Kay died, Prison Fellowship USA board member Chris Colson said: 'While serving six years of a 21-year prison sentence in a state prison for burglary, grand larceny and robbery, Mary Kay watched women gather soap, shampoo and toothpaste received from charity groups and wrap them as Christmas gifts for their children. She vowed she would do something for children who have an incarcerated parent when she was released from prison, and Prison Fellowship's Angel Tree programme is among her greatest legacies.'

Adapted from *Remembering an Angel*, 1st edition, Copyright © 2016-2017 by Prison Fellowship Ministries. Used with permission.
Angel Tree supports prisoners' family relationships by providing a way for them to give Christmas presents to their children. To find out more from Prison Fellowship visit www.prisonfellowship.org.uk

MARK 1:16-20

'One day Jesus was walking beside the Sea of Galilee. There he saw Simon and his brother Andrew. They were throwing a net into the lake. They were fishermen. "Come and follow me," Jesus said. "I will send you out to fish for people." At once they left their nets and followed him.

Then Jesus walked a little farther. As he did, he saw James, *the son of Zebedee, and his brother John. They were in a boat preparing their nets. Right away he called out to them. They left their father Zebedee in the boat with the hired men. Then they followed Jesus.'*

SOMETHING TO THINK ABOUT

Jesus called ordinary fishermen to follow him. He still calls ordinary men, women and children to follow him! Jesus' invitation to all of us today is, 'Come and follow me'. He invites us to be people who join his great task of telling the world about the good news he brings.

Mary Kay Beard, whose story you've just read, responded to God and became a follower of Jesus. God turned her life around. When she gave her life to God, he gave her work to do that has had an impact on thousands of prisoners and their families.

How will you respond to Jesus' invitation to follow him?

Prayer

Father in heaven, please give me your directions for my life. I want to follow you. Amen.

'I'm feeling terrible—I couldn't feel worse!
Get me on my feet again. You promised,
remember?...
Barricade the road that goes Nowhere;
grace me with your clear revelation.
I choose the true road to Somewhere,
I post your road signs at every curve and corner.
I grasp and cling to whatever you tell me;
GOD, don't let me down!
I'll run the course you lay out for me
if you'll just show me how.'
PSALM 119:25-32, *THE MESSAGE*

'"I know the plans I have for you," announces the
LORD. "I want you to enjoy success. I do not plan to
harm you. I will give you hope for the years to come.
Then you will call out to me. You will come and pray
to me. And I will listen to you. When you look for me
with all your heart, you will find me. I will be found by
you," announces the LORD.'
JEREMIAH 29:11-14

'Take the first step of faith. You don't have to see the
whole staircase, just take the first step.'
MARTIN LUTHER KING JR

04 Power to change

I was born in South Wales. Both my parents were Christians and my dad was a policeman so, from a very young age, I was taught good principles and values. But following the breakdown of my parents' marriage, and both of them later re-marrying other people, I ended up moving to Guernsey in the Channel Islands at the age of ten.

After getting a good education, I decided to pursue a career in finance, so I went to the local college to do a business and finance course. During my time at college I began to make choices that would set the path of the beginning of a ten-year journey of drugs, addiction and prison sentences.

It started with smoking cannabis at a friend's house at the age of 17, and it wasn't long before I was taking harder drugs like speed and ecstasy in night clubs. I began dealing drugs at 18 as I saw the potential to make a lot of money. Around this time, I had also secured a job as a trainee accountant. With a decent wage and extra income through selling ecstasy tablets, I was never short of money. The thing was, I was never satisfied – I always wanted more. I would constantly think of ways I could make money. My pursuit of wealth also took me down the road of gambling, an addiction that would eventually cost me hundreds of thousands of pounds.

Riddled with guilt

By my early twenties I was smuggling drugs – more profit for me, but more risk. This resulted in friends of mine going to prison, which hit me really hard as my choices were robbing people of their freedom. Seeing the devastation that I was causing, and the pain and hurt my family were going through because of the person I had become, I was riddled with guilt and shame.

What took away those feelings (temporarily) was heroin, and I became addicted to it at 23. Within a year I had lost everything – my job, my house, my health, friends, family – and then my freedom.

In June 2002 I was sentenced to four years for importing crack cocaine and heroin into Guernsey.

Being in prison gave me a lot of time to think about the choices I had made and the people I had hurt. I really wanted to change. My mum sent me books of stories of people who had been radically changed by God. I was moved by them. Then, one particular night in my cell, I began to cry out to God, asking for his forgiveness. That night I had an encounter with love that would change my life forever. God answered me. He forgave me and set me on a brand new path of healing, restoration and wholeness.

God's goodness

Fifteen years on, I have not stopped being in awe of God's goodness, kindness and faithfulness.

After leaving prison in 2004, I went on a Christian rehab programme for 16 months. During that time,

I experienced incredible healing from my past mistakes and my addictions, and God gave me clear direction for my future. Passionate about seeing broken lives restored, I had the privilege of working at the rehab for four years, and also became a chaplain for the elderly at a housing project my church ran. My passion to reach out to people in messed up situations and to share the love of Jesus took me to work for the charity Christians Against Poverty in 2009.

Contributed by Rod Williams. You can read more of Rod's story in his book, *The Real Deal* (Milton Keynes: Authentic, 2014). Used with permission.

 MARK 1:21-28

'Jesus and those with him went to Capernaum. When the Sabbath day came, he went into the synagogue. There he began to teach. The people were amazed at his teaching. That's because he taught them like one who had authority. He did not talk like the teachers of the law. Just then a man in their synagogue cried out. He was controlled by an evil spirit. He said, "What do you want with us, Jesus of Nazareth? Have you come to destroy us? I know who you are. You are the Holy One of God!"

"Be quiet!" said Jesus firmly. "Come out of him!" The evil spirit shook the man wildly. Then it came out of him with a scream.

All the people were amazed. So they asked each other, "What is this? A new teaching! And with so much authority! He even gives orders to evil spirits, and they obey him." News about Jesus spread quickly all over Galilee.'

SOMETHING TO THINK ABOUT

Jesus has the power and authority to confront evil in any form. What does evil look like in your world today?

Jesus' power means messed up lives can be sorted out. Mistakes can be overcome. Addictions can be broken. Are there areas of your life that need Jesus' hope and healing?

Prayer

Heavenly Father, thank you that you are more powerful than any evil I face. Please help me to trust you. I pray in Jesus' name. Amen.

'God gave us his Spirit. And the Spirit doesn't make us weak and fearful. Instead, the Spirit gives us power and love. He helps us control ourselves.'

2 TIMOTHY 1:7

Week 1 – Fresh start

As we continue reading, we will be getting to know Jesus better by reading his life story. We will also read how lives are changed when people get to know him.

We are taking a journey with Jesus from the River Jordan, where he was baptised, to the city of Jerusalem, where he was crucified and buried, and where he rose from the dead. The events happened 2,000 years ago, but you can still visit the places Jesus lived.

The prison stories in this book are up-to-date. They have been written about the hope found by people in the past few decades – almost all of them are still living today. As you read the stories and verses each day, ask God to speak to you about your life, and expect to hear from God through what you read. Each day, there's a story written about a prisoner, an ex-prisoner or a prison chaplain, as well as a few verses from the Bible.

If you are using this book daily during Lent, starting on Ash Wednesday, the 'Looking back, looking forward' sections are instead of a story and reading on a Sunday. And if you are part of a small group, these studies give the group questions to discuss.

You can read the short Bible sections included with the daily stories. Or if you prefer, you can read the whole chapters in Mark's Gospel to put the story into context.

READ: MARK CHAPTERS 1–3

Key verses

'At that time Jesus came from Nazareth in Galilee. John baptized Jesus in the Jordan River. Jesus was coming up out of the water. Just then he saw heaven being torn open. Jesus saw the Holy Spirit coming down on him like a dove. A voice spoke to him from heaven. It said, "You are my Son, and I love you. I am very pleased with you."

At once the Holy Spirit sent Jesus out into the desert. He was in the desert 40 days. There Satan tempted him. The wild animals didn't harm Jesus. Angels took care of him.'

Mark 1:9-13

THINK

1. Our relationships help to shape the people we become. Which relationships have shaped you for the better?

2. Looking at the description of Jesus' baptism, how would you describe Jesus' relationship with his Father in heaven?

3. When Jesus began preaching, he talked about the 'good news of God'. What does God's good news look like in your world? What is your experience of God's good news?

4. Jesus offers hope and healing. Where is this hope and healing needed today in your life or the lives of those around you?

LIFE LESSONS

1. When we become Christians, we are adopted into God's family. What difference would it make to your life to hear God say: 'You are my child, and I love you. I am very pleased with you'?

2. Jesus was tested and tempted. When we decide to follow Jesus we are tested and tempted too. What could you do to find the support you need to stay on course when life gets difficult?

3. In Mark's Gospel we see that Jesus gives his followers a new sense of purpose. What sense of purpose or direction has God given you? Is there a promise in the Bible that stands out for you?

4. Forgiveness is an important part of a Christian's journey. We accept God's forgiveness for all the wrong we have done, and we find freedom when we forgive others. What stops you forgiving others and receiving forgiveness?

LOOK AHEAD

In the first chapters of Mark's Gospel, Jesus' identity is being established. We see God fleshed out as a man who is tempted, just like we are tempted, but who doesn't sin. In the coming week, we will read about Jesus healing people, praying and partying. He had a clear sense of identity and purpose. Over the next few days, make a note of anything that surprises you about Jesus, or any questions you have about what you read.

The prison stories written for each day show that Jesus gives people the power to change. When someone's life is changed, they want others to discover God's love too. In one Bible story (Mark 2:1–12) we read that four friends made a hole in the roof of a building to lower a man to Jesus so he could be healed. Also, in one of the prison stories you will read this week, a prisoner escaped, but handed himself in at the police station when his ex-partner told him about Jesus' love and forgiveness.

Is there someone who needs you to introduce them to Jesus?

05 Jesus heals

I was born in Manchester to a very dysfunctional family. My parents are from Liverpool, and I was born in Salford in Manchester. Both my parents were alcoholics. They did the best they could with the tools that they had.

At the age of 15, I got into an argument between my mother and father. I came off worse, and got thrown out. I also got expelled from school at the same time for truancy, because I was bullied a lot.

I moved into a squat with some friends, and the guy who ran the 'gang' (if you want to call it that) became a bit of a role model for me. He took me under his wing and he looked after me. That got me involved in petty theft and crime. I was pathetic at it – I constantly got caught. That led to a relationship with the police, and eventually you know where that goes: prison.

Grizzly Risley

I went to Risley – nicknamed 'Grizzly Risley'. It was more of a detention, borstal-type centre. When I came out, I went to go home, but my parents were divorced, and someone else was living where I thought we lived. I tried to get myself together and took a couple of jobs. I worked in a bar at night and drove a truck by day to try to keep myself out of mischief, but I soon got bored.

I saw a poster for the Army. It was a very good marketing poster – it had two soldiers in camouflage uniform and a backdrop of snowy mountains. They were skiing, and it said, 'Do you want a life of adventure? Then join the British Army.' So I did, and I was sent to Northern Ireland. I didn't do much skiing! I did four tours in Northern Ireland, a tour of the Falklands and various other stuff. It was a great crew and I spent 16 years in the military. During that period, my work life was very good and I seemed to be a good soldier; I came out as a sergeant. But my private life was awful – two marriages, two divorces. I abandoned the child of my first marriage. I was drinking too much from being bullied. I got involved in boxing with the Army and became a bully in a uniform. That was my life, really – full of drink, divorce, debt and despair.

God's rescue plan

What changed? To cut a long story short, I did an Alpha course. God just completely hit me between the eyes and said, 'I love you. I want to rescue you. I want to help restore you, and I want to reintegrate you into a normal, healthy family.'

That's what he did. I became a Christian on the course, and it completely changed my life. I have been rescued. I am in the process of being restored, and I've been reintegrated into an amazing family – the Church. My Christian friends have supported me, engaged with me, knocked some of the rough edges off me and have given me hope that I can change.

Contributed by Rev Paul Cowley MBE, who was ordained in 2002 and is the founder and CEO of Caring for Ex-offenders. He pioneered Alpha in prisons. His story is used with permission.

MARK 1:29-34

'Jesus and those with him left the synagogue. Right away they went with James and John to the home of Simon and Andrew. Simon's mother-in-law was lying in bed with a fever. They told Jesus about her right away. So he went to her. He took her hand and helped her up. The fever left her. Then she began to serve them.

That evening after sunset, the people brought to Jesus all who were sick. They also brought all who were controlled by demons. All the people in town gathered at the door. Jesus healed many of them. They had all kinds of sicknesses. He also drove out many demons. But he would not let the demons speak, because they knew who he was.'

SOMETHING TO THINK ABOUT

Jesus has the power to heal lives, whatever the source of our sickness. Mark describes how Jesus made a difference to the lives of the people he met. He welcomed everyone, whatever their problem.

He still wants to do the same today. Sometimes there's an instant change, a miraculous healing. Sometimes Jesus is at work through the medical profession. Sometimes he works in ways that we don't understand, and the outcome isn't as we expect. But always, he is ready to reach out to welcome us, to show us how much we are loved.

Jesus is the ultimate role model. He invites us to work with him and says, 'Anyone who believes in me will do the works I have been doing' (John 14:12).

Prayer

Father in heaven, reach out today to touch my life and the lives of those I love and pray for. Please do this for Jesus' sake. Amen.

'May the God who gives hope fill you with great joy. May you have perfect peace as you trust in him. May the power of the Holy Spirit fill you with hope.'

ROMANS 15:13

'Fear imprisons, faith liberates; fear paralyses, faith empowers; fear disheartens, faith encourages; fear sickens, faith heals; fear makes useless, faith makes serviceable.'

HARRY EMERSON FOSDICK

06 Finding hope

When I was asked to write my personal testimony, I immediately thought of *The Divine Comedy* by Dante, and the words that are written above his gates of hell: 'Abandon hope all ye who enter here'.

Many think of prison as being like hell, and they feel that hope has abandoned them. But I would say it was the complete opposite for me. Before I was sentenced, I had forgotten about hope and my Christian heritage. I was doing vast amounts of heroin and crack, and that consumed my waking moments. It wasn't until I was told by the judge that I would be receiving a custodial sentence that I started to look seriously at where I was in life.

Help needed

Did I want to waste my time in prison and then return to the same life that I had left? I didn't want that at all, so I decided to use prison as rehab – not only to get clean from all the drugs, but to re-educate myself, and also better myself personally.

There were a lot of obstacles in my way. I had no family on the outside so I had no support structure at all. I realised I couldn't do it on my own. I needed support, and the only one who would and could support me was there with me all along. So one night, before my sentencing, I asked God to guide me through this ordeal and asked him to help me in any way he could. I never expected anything to change – after all, I'd prayed many times in the past and I didn't see any benefit in it. But this time it was different.

As soon as I entered the prison system, things started to happen for me. I always ended up with a good job. I managed to do enough re-education in English, maths and business studies and all the courses that go hand in hand with them. I was already reaping the benefits of prayer, so I got a lot bolder and started attending chapel services regularly.

Life changed

Then I started praying for all sorts of things. Every time I placed my life in the hands of Jesus and let him guide me, things just seemed to work out for me. I worried less about the stuff I couldn't change. I relaxed more and began to enjoy my own company again. I was beginning to feel good about myself. I was becoming a new person. I felt washed clean. I no longer craved drugs. I was less aggressive. My life had changed. But could I maintain this way of living? All I had was hope, so I kept on hoping and praying. Every time I moved to a new prison, I seemed to find like-minded people who were also on a journey to change their lives.

Now I only have a few months left of my sentence, and I am still full of hope. I have a job to go to thanks to the Halfords Academy and the training I am being given at the moment. Everything is looking up for me. The future is the brightest I have ever known. So, for me, hope wasn't abandoned at the gates of prison. It was the start of it. I found that hope in prayer and the teachings of Jesus. For me, prison was a lesson in change. All I needed was hope and I got that at every turn. Hope is the key to the prison gates. Hope is what keeps us going.

Contributed by a prisoner.

MARK 1:35-38

'It was very early in the morning and still dark. Jesus got up and left the house. He went to a place where he could be alone. There he prayed. Simon and his friends went to look for Jesus. When they found him, they called out, "Everyone is looking for you!"

Jesus replied, "Let's go somewhere else. I want to go to the nearby towns. I must preach there also. That is why I have come."'

SOMETHING TO THINK ABOUT

Prayer was a vital part of Jesus' life. He wanted to spend time talking to his heavenly Father, alone. As we pray we can place our lives into Jesus' hands to let him guide us. We don't need to use holy words or a holy voice. Our heavenly Father delights in welcoming us just as we are. As we talk to him, we can expect God to speak to us – often through what we read in his Word, the Bible.

What is God saying to you today?

Prayer

When Jesus' followers asked him how to pray, he give them a simple pattern that we have come to describe as The Lord's Prayer:

> *Our Father in heaven,*
> *hallowed be your name,*
> *your kingdom come,*
> *your will be done,*
> *on earth as in heaven.*
> *Give us today our daily bread.*
> *Forgive us our sins*
> *as we forgive those who sin against us.*
> *Lead us not into temptation*
> *but deliver us from evil.*
> *For the kingdom, the power,*
> *and the glory are yours*
> *now and for ever.*
> *Amen.*

'Forgive other people when they sin against you. If you do, your Father who is in heaven will also forgive you. But if you do not forgive the sins of other people, your Father will not forgive your sins.'

MATTHEW 6:14-15

07 The hand of God

Something happened to me when I was 18 months old. We are not entirely sure what the abuse was, but it left me unable to process emotion without twitching. As a result, I grew up conscious that people looked at me differently. I lacked confidence, struggled at school and was left with low self-esteem.

At the age of ten, having attended a Christian gathering called Spring Harvest, I asked Jesus to come into my heart – at least, if he was able to open the door, because I felt unable to. But I knew something had happened; that God had his hand on my life in a special way. The road ahead should have destroyed me, but God had other plans.

At 12 years old, I was befriended by a paedophile. I was groomed and sexually abused and exploited by him until I was 17, when I managed to walk away. I thought it was all my fault, until flashbacks started occurring. My silence would last another decade.

Troubled past

I went on to work with people with emotional and behavioural difficulties, and through a God-orchestrated set of events, found myself married and needing to deal with my past. I broke the silence, went to the police, and through the courts I saw the perpetrator go to prison for a substantial period of time.

Then God called me into ministry, and I led a couple of churches. During this time, he impacted my life with the 'Luke 4 Manifesto':

'The Spirit of the Lord is on me,
because he has anointed me
to proclaim good news to the poor.
He has sent me to proclaim freedom for
the prisoners
and recovery of sight for the blind,
to set the oppressed free,
to proclaim the year of the Lord's favour.'
(Luke 4:18–19, NIV)

I started to mix more with those on the streets and found the majority of them had prison backgrounds; pasts that they felt unable to escape; baggage that chained them. It was for these people Jesus came. So I stepped out from church ministry and sought to work with ex-offenders, starting by linking with the local prison.

Hope restored

I now work entirely inside prisons as a chaplain. What a strange turnaround in life when God uses the abused to minister to the abuser! When Jesus declares the kingdom of God is near to the offender and the modern-day lepers, he uses love and acceptance rather than judgment and rejection, and hope is restored.

God is a master at this stuff. He takes the unconfident, bruised and beaten, the abused and hopeless, neglected and manipulated child on a journey, led by his hand through a redemptive circle towards wholeness. Then he uses that child of his, years later, to bring good news to the poor, to bring true freedom to the prisoner, to bring healing to the damaged, to bring freedom to the oppressed in Jesus' name.

Contributed by a prison chaplain.

MARK 1:40-42

'A man who had a skin disease came to Jesus. On his knees he begged Jesus. He said, "If you are willing to make me 'clean,' you can do it."

Jesus became angry. He reached out his hand and touched the man. "I am willing to do it," Jesus said. "Be 'clean'!" Right away the disease left the man, and he was "clean."'

SOMETHING TO THINK ABOUT

Jesus knows just what we need. This man with the skin disease would have been an outcast. No one would want to touch him. Imagine how important it was for him to have Jesus touch him. Jesus healed him physically, and that touch must have brought emotional healing too.

Today's prison story said: 'When Jesus declares the kingdom of God is near to the offender and the modern-day lepers, he uses love and acceptance rather than judgment and rejection, and hope is restored.'

When you pray 'Your kingdom come', what change are you expecting in your own life and in the lives of those around you?

Prayer

There are many prayers in the Bible. For example you can
read this psalm as a prayer and make it your own:
'I call out to the LORD when I'm in trouble,
and he answers me.
LORD, save me from people whose lips tell lies.
Save me from people whose tongues don't tell the truth.'
(Psalm 120:1-2)
Amen.

'Don't you know who made everything?
Haven't you heard about him?
The LORD is the God who lives forever.
He created everything on earth.
He won't become worn out or get tired.
No one will ever know how great his
understanding is.
He gives strength to those who are tired.
He gives power to those who are weak.
Even young people become worn out and get tired.
Even the best of them trip and fall.
But those who trust in the LORD
will receive new strength.
They will fly as high as eagles.
They will run and not get tired.
They will walk and not grow weak.'

ISAIAH 40:28-31

08 Jesus gives hope

'Our job is to give people hope,' says the Rev Patrick Wright. He's one of the chaplains at Heathrow's Immigration Removal Centre. Here, roughly a thousand men and a couple of dozen women are awaiting news of when and if they will be deported from the UK.

The reasons could be many and various: overstaying a visa, having arrived in the UK illegally, having committed a crime, or simply, in the case of the people that we meet, having made a series of mistakes.

Source of hope

'It definitely is a place where a lot of people feel hopeless,' Patrick says. 'We see lots of low-level depression here. But,' he adds, 'the Gospels bring hope.' And so it is that Patrick and his colleagues are giving away at least 50 Bibles a year to detainees in a vast range of languages, from Farsi to Tamil, Urdu to Nepalese. And they keep their chapel stocked with a good supply of Bibles so that anyone can drop by and read them.

Some of the people Patrick works with remain in detention, in a state of uncertainty, sometimes for as long as a year. In the end, three quarters will be deported. Patrick is aware of the perilous future awaiting some detainees.

Hopeful stories

'We've got people who have come to know Jesus while in the UK. We have a couple of guys from Africa whose families are involved in witchcraft and want them to take over. Some are genuinely fearful,' Patrick says. 'I see this as a mission field, a place that God has called me to. My role is to impart hope. And the Bible is full of hopeful stories: my favourite is the story of Joseph, where at the end he is able to look back and say, "God was in it." I have to give a genuinely biblical hope, which isn't that life will be without pain or sorrow, but that we can see God's purposes for us, even if it means walking a difficult path and facing choices that we would rather not make.'

Contributed by Bible Society. Used with permission.

JOSEPH'S STORY

Joseph had ten older brothers, but he was his dad's favourite son. That made the others jealous. They plotted to kill him, but sold him to slave traders instead. The slave traders took him to Egypt where he ended up in prison. Later in life, the tables were turned and his brothers came to him begging. They feared for their lives, but Joseph forgave them and said: 'Don't be afraid... You planned to harm me. But God planned it for good.' (You can read Joseph's story in Genesis 30–50.)

MARK 2:1-12

'A few days later, Jesus entered Capernaum again. The people heard that he had come home. So many people gathered that there was no room left. There was not even room outside the door. And Jesus preached the word to them.

Four of those who came were carrying a man who could not walk. But they could not get him close to Jesus because of the crowd. So they made a hole by digging through the roof above Jesus. Then they lowered the man through it on a mat. Jesus saw their faith. So he said to the man, "Son, your sins are forgiven."

Some teachers of the law were sitting there. They were thinking, "Why is this fellow talking like that? He's saying a very evil thing! Only God can forgive sins!"

Right away Jesus knew what they were thinking. So he said to them, "Why are you thinking these things? Is it easier to say to this man, 'Your sins are forgiven'? Or to say, 'Get up, take your mat and walk'? But I want you to know that the Son of Man has authority on earth to forgive sins." So Jesus spoke to the man who could not walk. "I tell you," he said, "get up. Take your mat and go home." The man got up and took his mat. Then he walked away while everyone watched. All the people were amazed. They praised God and said, "We have never seen anything like this!"'

SOMETHING TO THINK ABOUT

When Jesus said, 'Son, your sins are forgiven', the religious leaders were outraged. Jesus was claiming to do something only God can do. Of course, Jesus is God in human form, so he has the authority to forgive sin. He proved that to his critics by healing the paralysed man.

The four friends in today's Bible story were determined to bring their friend to Jesus, so they dug a hole in the roof over Jesus' head. Who do you want to bring to Jesus today? Who needs the hope that only Jesus can give?

Prayer

Thank you, Jesus, that you have the authority to forgive sins and the power to heal lives. I am praying today for... [list the people you are praying for]. I bring them to you and ask that you will do them good today and give them fresh hope. I am praying this in your name, Jesus. Amen.

'We know that in all things God works for the good of those who love him. He appointed them to be saved in keeping with his purpose.'
ROMANS 8:28

09 Changed for good

Growing up wasn't very nice for me, and for my mum it was nothing but a struggle. We lived in a small two-bedroomed terraced house with no bathroom – only an outside toilet – and a shower in my bedroom. I've never met my father, but from what I've been told, he was a heroin addict. My mum had to let him go because he wouldn't change. This was very hard for her and put a lot of pressure on her to provide, and so she began to shoplift. My mum wasn't a drug addict or an alcoholic; she just did what she had to do to put food on the table and clothes on my back. There were many times when I can remember my mum getting arrested for shoplifting.

Breaking up, breaking down

My mum had a few relationships, but none of those men wanted to take on someone else's kid. Then 'Mr Right' came along, someone to take care of me and love my mum. Unfortunately, it didn't last. My mum had a mental breakdown and blamed me for the break up.

I became so angry inside and told myself I would never trust anyone again. I started to get in trouble at school hanging around with the kids who smoked cannabis and went shoplifting. That's how it all started.

At first I thought what I was doing was cool, but it soon got out of control. At the age of 14 I was injecting amphetamines, and my drug-taking didn't stop there.

It escalated to heroin and crack cocaine, and my crimes went from shoplifting to breaking into shops and homes and eventually to armed robbery.

Inside

Because of my crimes, I've spent a total of 11 years in prison. I became institutionalised, thinking I was better off in prison and believing I could never change. But then came a dramatic event in my life. I was doing six years for armed robbery and got my D Cat*, which is open prison. I was hooked on heroin and smoking cannabis. I can remember thinking to myself, 'Why am I like this?' and 'Why can't I change?' At that moment, I heard a voice in my head say, 'This is what you are. This is all you will ever be.' With that I escaped from prison, stole a car, and went to see my ex-partner.

She let me in and we started talking. She told me that she had become a Christian, and that God loved me and could change my life if I would ask him into my heart. She told me that God wanted to forgive my past, and that is why Jesus died on the cross.

Police Station

That night, I thought about what she had said. I was sick of my life and wanted to change, but knew I couldn't do it on my own. The next day I handed myself in at the police station, and they took me to Lincoln prison. When I arrived, I put my name down for chapel. The next day, I went to chapel and gave my life to Jesus.

A new start

That was five years ago. Now I help bring hope, love, and restoration into broken lives working as senior support worker. My wife and I have a daughter, and God has restored my relationship with my son despite the eight years of his life I spent in prison. I now see him on a regular basis. God has blessed me with a great mentor, who has opened the doors for me to share my story to others in prison, telling them the good news of Jesus and what he can do in their lives.

Contributed by an ex-offender.

*Prisoners at 'D Cat' are, subject to approval, given release on temporary licence to work in the community, or go on 'home leave' once they have passed their full licence eligibility dates (usually a quarter of the way through the sentence).

MARK 2:15-17

'Later Jesus was having dinner at Levi's house. Many tax collectors and sinners were eating with him and his disciples. They were part of the large crowd following Jesus. Some teachers of the law who were Pharisees were there. They saw Jesus eating with sinners and tax collectors. So they asked his disciples, "Why does he eat with tax collectors and sinners?"

Jesus heard that. So he said to them, "Those who are healthy don't need a doctor. Sick people do. I have not come to get those who think they are right with God to follow me. I have come to get sinners to follow me."'

SOMETHING TO THINK ABOUT

Levi was one of Jesus' newest followers. He wanted his friends to know Jesus too, so he invited them all to a meal. Jesus wanted to be with the people who needed to hear his good news. Do you have friends or family members who need to discover how much Jesus loves them?

Prayer

Lord Jesus, have mercy on me. Help me. Make me strong to face what each day holds. Save me. Amen.

'So turn away from your sins. Turn to God. Then your sins will be wiped away. The time will come when the Lord will make everything new.'

ACTS 3:19

10 Rebuilding relationships

I was in prison in 2014 when I saw a green flyer on a noticeboard that said, 'Caring for Ex-Offenders'. They claimed that they could link you to a local church in an area, and help you with employment and housing. So I wrote these people a letter. We were writing back and forth, but they needed to know where I was going to be situated before they could link me with a church.

It was getting close to my release date and I was so scared. I really didn't want to go back to Bristol where I was brought up. Everyone I knew was in addiction – family members, friends – I had nothing to occupy my time. My daughter was living in Wales. I had loads of conditions that restricted where I could go in Bristol. In all honesty, once out I just wanted to go back to prison.

Finding hope

I had been in a Bristol probation bail hostel for a few months and had started drinking again, but not heavily. I was not banned from drinking, but I wasn't allowed to 'blow over 35' (the drink-driving breathalyser limit). I remember telling my key worker that my drinking was going to get out of hand. I recall sitting down on the pavement one day with a can of beer and I just broke down, sobbing. I could see that my life was going to deteriorate again through drink and drugs.

A few days later I was told by the hostel that someone had been in contact with probation and wanted to meet me. His name was Silas, and he was a pastor of a church called Hope Chapel. I discovered from Silas that Caring for Ex-offenders had contacted him and asked if he would meet up with me. When we met, Silas gave me directions to his church, which also ran a foodbank that day. The church was about a mile and a half away. After I had met Silas, I bumped into three people who asked if they could pray for me. I said I was in a bit of a rush, but they prayed for me anyway. I went back to the hostel, got my bike and cycled to Hope Chapel.

New connections

When I got to Hope Chapel I was given some food by the foodbank, and some people chatted to me. I didn't find it easy to chat, but meeting these new people was vital in keeping me away from my old life. I was told that there was a recovery group in the church every Wednesday, and I was eager to see what that was about, so I got involved straight away. Then I linked up with MentorMe. By engaging with positive people, I was able to keep away from my old haunts. With the help of MentorMe I can now be around family members, even if they are still in addiction, but I am strong enough for it not to adversely affect me.

I have now re-established my relationship with my daughter. I travel to Wales every weekend to pick her up and she comes to stay with me, which makes me feel brilliant. I am able to be a daddy as much as I can. I am also slowly rebuilding a relationship with my dad, which I have never found easy. But the Man Up course that I am doing, which is run by one of the churches, is really helping me to do this.

One of the guys at Hope is now mentoring an old childhood friend of mine who has also been in prison and addiction. We are able to encourage one another. I have now done the training course with MentorMe so I can mentor others. I have some work as well, driving care worker staff to addresses where they are able to care for elderly, disabled, and vulnerable people.

Contributed by an ex-offender.

MentorMe is a Bristol-based project that mentors men and women coming out of prison and relocating in the Bristol area. The mentors come from local Bristol churches.

 MARK 3:31–35

'Jesus' mother and brothers came and stood outside. They sent someone in to get him. A crowd was sitting around Jesus. They told him, "Your mother and your brothers are outside. They are looking for you."

"Who is my mother? Who are my brothers?" he asked.

Then Jesus looked at the people sitting in a circle around him. He said, "Here is my mother! Here are my brothers! Anyone who does what God wants is my brother or sister or mother."'

SOMETHING TO THINK ABOUT

As Christians we are adopted into God's family. It's a family that links us with millions of Jesus' followers throughout history and around the world. One day, countless numbers of people from every tribe and nation will stand before God, worshipping him (Revelation 7:9).

Prayer

Dear God, thank you for making it possible for me to know you as my Father. I am sorry for ignoring you sometimes. Please help me to follow your Son Jesus. Amen.

'Give praise to the Lord.
Give praise to God our Savior.
He carries our heavy loads day after day.
Our God is a God who saves.
He is the King and the LORD.
He saves us from death.'

PSALM 68:19–20

Week 2 – Authority established

Jesus grew up in a Middle-Eastern town called Nazareth. You can still visit it in modern-day Israel. He was known as a carpenter's son. His baptism was the turning point in his life. That's when his identity as God's Son was revealed. From then on he travelled throughout the country preaching, teaching and healing people, showing people what God is like.

He chose a group of 12 followers (disciples) and showed them how they could live God's way and trust him for everything. He is still calling people to follow him today and he promises to be with us always and everywhere.

Jesus gave his followers his authority to do the things he had been doing. He invites his modern-day followers to co-operate with him too. He even says we will do the work he did (John 14:12).

But not everyone accepted Jesus. They couldn't accept that he was sent by God. They were amazed at his teaching, but they didn't put their faith in him. Their lack of faith limited what Jesus could do among them.

READ: MARK CHAPTERS 4–6

Key verses

'He called the 12 disciples to him. Then he began to send them out two by two. He gave them authority to drive out evil spirits.

Here is what he told them to do. "Take only a walking stick for your trip. Do not take bread or a bag. Take no money in your belts. Wear sandals. But do not take extra clothes. When you are invited into a house, stay there until you leave town. Some places may not welcome you or listen to you. If they don't, leave that place and shake the dust off your feet. That will be a witness against the people living there."

They went out. And they preached that people should turn away from their sins. They drove out many demons. They poured olive oil on many sick people and healed them.'
Mark 6:7–13

THINK

1. First, discuss any questions you have about what you have read in the past week.

2. What have your learned about Jesus in the past week? What surprises you about him?

3. Jesus got up early to pray, and he taught his followers a simple pattern for prayer. When and where do you pray?

4. In the Bible stories we have read, Jesus meets many different people: Simon's mother-in-law, who is sick;

a man with a skin disease, who was probably an outcast from society as a result; a paralysed man lowered through a roof on a mat to meet him; tax collectors, sinners and religious people at Levi's house. Which of the people Jesus meets do you identify with?

5. In Mark chapters 4–6, Jesus shows his authority by stopping a storm, feeding thousands of people, and walking on water. He gave his disciples authority and sent them out to preach as he had been doing. Do you talk to other people about Jesus and what it means to follow him? What is the reaction of the people you talk to?

LIFE LESSONS

1. What have you learned from the prison stories that we've read in the past week?

2. Role models can play an important part in shaping our lives. Who are the good role models who have helped to shape your life?

3. Prayer has made a difference to the lives of prisoners and ex-prisoners in this week's stories. What is your experience of prayer?

4. An Alpha course, the shock of a custodial sentence, getting married... There are several different turning points mentioned in the prison stories we have read this week. Has there been a turning point in your life, when you have found hope? Give time to sharing these stories in the group.

LOOK AHEAD

- During the next week, use the prayer Jesus taught his followers (Luke 11:2–4) as a pattern to write a prayer.
- In the coming week we will read how Jesus' true identity is revealed. Think about the way people in Nazareth, Jesus' home town, reacted to him. Will you be like them, or will you put your faith in Jesus?
- What is stopping you being wholehearted as a follower of Jesus? Will you trust him to give you everything you need?
- If you are already a follower of Jesus, pray for the people you know who are not yet his followers. Ask God to speak to them and reveal himself to them.
- Pray too for yourself. Ask for God's help and his peace.

11 Trusting Jesus

Abdul met Jesus in a dream while awaiting deportation at Heathrow.

'I came to the UK because I had a problem in Afghanistan,' says Abdul. That's a bit of an under-statement, as it turns out. Abdul was being held at Heathrow's Immigration Removal Centre awaiting deportation. And it was there that he discovered the Bible.

'I committed adultery with my neighbour's wife,' he says. 'The father of the man came and I ran away, because in Afghanistan, when you commit adultery, they will kill you. I was afraid that I would be killed.'

Abdul fled to his uncle's house in Kabul. There he paid $6,000 to a trafficker to bring him to the UK in the back of a lorry. This was ten years ago.

For four years he sofa-surfed and lived a hand-to-mouth existence. Then, in 2011, he was stopped randomly by the police. This led to them discovering that he had no legal status in the UK, and so he found himself at Heathrow awaiting deportation.

Befriended

There he was befriended by a Nigerian Christian detainee who introduced Abdul to the Bible. After reading it one night, Abdul had a dream.

'It was 4.30am,' he says. 'All the world was very dark, but then a person appeared, shining like light. I couldn't look at his face. I said, "Who are you?" He said, "I am Jesus, the Messiah." I said, "Who are all these other people?" He said, "These are all the people who love me." And then I woke up. I couldn't sleep. I stood and thought about it, and then I came to the chapel. I think that Jesus is my friend to tell me about himself like that.'

Abdul started reading a Bible in his native language. 'The Bible gives me everything I need really,' he says. 'When I read it I become relaxed and I forget that I'm in the detention centre. It makes me very happy.'

Contributed by Bible Society. Used with permission.

MARK 4:35-41

'When evening came, Jesus said to his disciples, "Let's go over to the other side of the lake." They left the crowd behind. And they took him along in a boat, just as he was. There were also other boats with him. A wild storm came up. Waves crashed over the boat. It was about to sink. Jesus was in the back, sleeping on a cushion. The disciples woke him up. They said, "Teacher! Don't you care if we drown?"

He got up and ordered the wind to stop. He said to the waves, "Quiet! Be still!" Then the wind died down. And it was completely calm.

He said to his disciples, "Why are you so afraid? Don't you have any faith at all yet?"

They were terrified. They asked each other, "Who is this? Even the wind and the waves obey him!"'

SOMETHING TO THINK ABOUT

Jesus' disciples had a lot to learn. When a storm threatened to sink their boat, they focused on their dangerous circumstances, instead of trusting that Jesus was in control. When life is stormy and difficult, it is not always easy to trust Jesus with our lives. But God has said, 'I will never leave you. I will never desert you.' So, like the first Christians, we can say boldly, 'The Lord helps me. I will not be afraid' (Hebrews 13:5-6).

What difficult circumstances are you facing? Will you trust Jesus, whatever happens?

Prayer

Make this psalm a prayer for yourself:
Father God,
'How can I get away from your Spirit?
Where can I go to escape from you?
If I go up to the heavens, you are there.
If I lie down in the deepest parts of the earth, you are also there.
Suppose I were to rise with the sun in the east.
Suppose I travel to the west where it sinks into the ocean.
Your hand would always be there to guide me.
Your right hand would still be holding me close.'
(Psalm 139:7-10)
Thank you. Help me to trust you with my whole life. Amen.

'I will pour out my Spirit on all people.
Your sons and daughters will prophesy.
Your old men will have dreams.
Your young men will have visions.
In those days I will pour out my Spirit
on those who serve me, men and
women alike.'

JOEL 2:28-29

'The word of God is alive and active. It is
sharper than any sword that has two edges.
It cuts deep enough to separate soul from
spirit. It can separate bones from joints. It
judges the thoughts and purposes of the
heart. Nothing God created is hidden from
him. His eyes see everything. He will hold us
responsible for everything we do.'

HEBREWS 4:12-13

12 Don't be afraid... <u>believe</u>

Hope isn't a word I've used much in my life; neither is it something I have often felt. Sometimes life can be very hard and we may never understand why we experience such hardships, often blaming ourselves and others. Other times life can just overwhelm us, and we feel lost.

I was conceived when my drunk father violated my mother. I didn't find out until my dad died and the funeral was over. My sisters told me; my mother confirmed it. Grief-stricken at my dad dying, age 58, having cared for him during his short illness, I felt inconsolable, lost, dead to the world, defective, dirty and abnormal. I was 20 years old.

Trying to comfort myself with alcohol, sex, lies and gambling, I racked up thousands of pounds of credit card debt to make life better. There was nothing I could do to change my life; nothing to change how I'd been conceived or repair what had been done. My father had abused me and my sisters during our childhoods and I hated him. My anger, resentment and revenge was being misdirected, and my life was chaotic. I have held on to the guilt and shame of what my father did for many years, causing the sadness, depression, self-harm, flashbacks and lack of boundaries around others.

I am a survivor

The guilt, shame and anger are gone now. I want you to know that I am a survivor – no longer a victim. I have forgiven my father. I am very blessed that God has enabled doctors, therapists, nurses and psychologists to help me understand my feelings, emotions and thought processes. God has healed me by his Holy Spirit and the work of those kind professionals.

Last time I self-harmed was February 2015. Last time I hurt anyone was May 2011. It has been possible for me to have closure and to be healed. I don't feel cut off from the world anymore. There is hope in prison. There are more and more opportunities for therapy, treatment, care and progression. That is hope. As I write these words from my jail cell, continuing my therapy pathway and working hard, I am thinking of you, the reader, praying for hope and healing for you. You are not alone. Jesus never turned anyone away. He welcomed everyone, no matter how bad, messed up, abused, defective, socially abnormal, addicted, abusive, murderous, perverse or odd. He welcomes you today, just as you are.

Contributed by a prisoner.

'Be strong, all you who put your hope in the LORD. Never give up.'

PSALM 31:24

MARK 5:22-24,35-36,38-42

'*A man named Jairus came. He was a synagogue leader. When he saw Jesus, he fell at his feet. He begged Jesus, "Please come. My little daughter is dying. Place your hands on her to heal her. Then she will live." So Jesus went with him...*

While Jesus was still speaking, some people came from the house of Jairus... "Your daughter is dead," they said. "Why bother the teacher anymore?"

Jesus heard what they were saying. He told the synagogue leader, "Don't be afraid. Just believe."...

They came to the home of the synagogue leader. There Jesus saw a lot of confusion. People were crying and sobbing loudly. He went inside. Then he said to them, "Why all this confusion and sobbing? The child is not dead. She is only sleeping." But they laughed at him.

He made them all go outside. He took only the child's father and mother and the disciples who were with him. And he went in where the child was. He took her by the hand. Then he said to her, "Talitha koum!" This means, "Little girl, I say to you, get up!" The girl was 12 years old. Right away she stood up and began to walk around.'

SOMETHING TO THINK ABOUT

Jairus was a religious leader in Jerusalem about 2,000 years ago. His colleagues were out to get Jesus. But Jairus was desperate. His daughter was dying. Jesus was his only hope, so he risked his reputation to ask Jesus to help. As a result, the girl was restored to her family.

Jesus is still in the business of restoring lives. Are there aspects of your life that need to change? Is Jesus saying to you: 'Don't be afraid. Just believe' – the same words he said to Jairus?

Prayer

Dear God, I want to believe that I can trust you. Please help me. Amen.

'Are you tired? Worn out? Burned out on religion? Come to me. Get away with me and you'll recover your life. I'll show you how to take a real rest. Walk with me and work with me—watch how I do it. Learn the unforced rhythms of grace. I won't lay anything heavy or ill-fitting on you. Keep company with me and you'll learn how to live freely and lightly.'

MATTHEW 11:18-20, *THE MESSAGE*

13 <u>Survivor</u>

It was my 16th birthday. I was at my friend's house, and there were lots of drugs around. I had been sexually abused from the age of 12 by my cousin and his friends, and I could no longer handle the pain I was going through – so I turned to drink and drugs. Getting high helped me to forget. But then I became addicted, and that meant I needed money. I was running around Wigan carrying out robberies, stealing whatever I could to pay for my next fix. I was consistently getting into gangs and owing dealers, and I was in and out of the police station every week.

Then I relocated to Manchester. I remember once getting on a train with a sawn-off shotgun shoved up my top, and then I walked to my sister's house. She went crazy, screaming at me to get the gun out of her house.

Desperate and in debt

I was desperate to make a fresh start, but ended up even deeper in the drug scene. I started dealing to pay for my habit, but just ended up in debt with my so-called friends. So I went back into robbery.

Inevitably, I eventually got arrested and ended up doing six months in Hindley and Stoke Heath prisons.

When I got out, I really wanted to change, but just went back to my old ways. I tried to sort my life out, but it didn't work; I just ended up with another prison sentence.

I was depressed and self-harming, and put on a 24-hour suicide watch in the prison hospital wing. With no drink or drugs inside me, all the feelings of being abused as a child came flooding back.

I remember the day in HMP Forest Bank when my cell door opened and a sweet old lady came in; a prison chaplain named Beryl. 'I have been told you want to harm yourself,' she said. All I could do was cry.

Learning to forgive

Something came with Beryl that day. Now I know it was the Holy Spirit. She told me that Jesus took all my pain, hurt and anger to the cross. Jesus went through being cut and bruised for me, and that meant I didn't need to do it to myself. It was the first time I had been able to tell anyone what I had been through.

That day I asked Jesus into my life, and things started to change. After my release, I moved to Rochdale, where I loved going to church. It wasn't easy though – the pain of my past kept me dabbling in drugs. Then my sister died. She was 29 years old and had died from drinking too much. I started to blame God, and hit the bottle hard. I was taking drugs and self-harming. But I knew I couldn't go on like this.

I went to a Christian rehab centre, and it was in that place I learned to forgive. I forgave the people who had abused me. I'm not a victim anymore. I am a survivor in Jesus Christ.

Contributed by an ex-offender.

MARK 6:1-6

'Jesus left there and went to his hometown of Nazareth. His disciples went with him. When the Sabbath day came, he began to teach in the synagogue. Many who heard him were amazed.

"Where did this man get these things?" they asked. "What's this wisdom that has been given to him? What are these remarkable miracles he is doing? Isn't this the carpenter? Isn't this Mary's son? Isn't this the brother of James, Joseph, Judas and Simon? Aren't his sisters here with us?" They were not pleased with him at all.

Jesus said to them, "A prophet is honored everywhere except in his own town. He doesn't receive any honor among his relatives or in his own home." Jesus placed his hands on a few sick people and healed them. But he could not do any other miracles there. He was amazed because they had no faith.'

SOMETHING TO THINK ABOUT

Jesus was rejected by the people in his own home town. The negative atmosphere had an impact. But, as today's story shows, a change of location doesn't always solve our problems. We need a change of heart – the type of change that only God can do, when his Holy Spirit comes to live in us. Holding on to unforgiveness blocks change too. Forgiving others, as God forgives us, releases us from the past. Then we can make a fresh start.

Prayer

Thank you, Father God, for forgiving me.
Please help me to forgive others. Amen.

'LORD, who is a God like you?
You forgive sin.
You forgive your people
when they do what is wrong.
You don't stay angry forever.
Instead, you take delight in showing
your faithful love to them.'

MICAH 7:18-19

'When anyone lives in Christ, the new
creation has come. The old is gone!
The new is here!'

2 CORINTHIANS 5:17

'God creates out of nothing. Wonderful,
you say. Yes, to be sure, but he does what
is still more wonderful: he makes saints
out of sinners.'

SØREN KIERKEGAARD

14 Back to basics

Hopelessness gripped me the moment I was put into prison as a young man. I tried hard to outwardly cover my fear and anxiety, but inside I was crumbling. I felt numb, resigned and accepting of my incarceration, but my outer bravado masked the inner turmoil I was feeling.

Nights were when I felt most alone. Lost in my own thoughts, I would lie awake for hours imagining life outside – meals I would eat, walks I could go on, friends I could talk to – but soon the cries of other prisoners would jolt me back to reality. I started to sleep with my head under a pillow to drown out the noise of the heroin addicts throwing all they could against their cell doors, while screaming for a fix that was never coming.

Doubt and deals

The pillow drowned out the exterior noise, but it also drove me deeper into my interior self; sending me back and forth between the dream of beautiful things and the nightmare of being locked up.

I don't know quite when it happened, but eventually I started to pray – like an inner mental dialogue with a creator I hoped might be listening. I would do deals with him; make promises; ask for help – I was focused almost entirely on myself.

Then the doubt crept in that maybe I had just developed an imaginary friend. Was I going mad? Was I just talking to myself? Questions, anxiety and fear slipped in; the long nights slowly passed in mental turmoil until, eventually, I would slip into a deep blackness somewhere under my pillow. Every morning I would wake up feeling exhausted and drained, trying to shake off the fears of the night by engaging in the monotony of the day. It became cyclical – every night under my pillow, the dialogue would continue. Yet this 'god' I had apparently made up never seemed to help.

Unlikely peace

One night, I was alone in my cell and the sleeplessness and anxiety were overwhelming. There was no peace, only a storm in my head. But then it happened. This time, I spoke out loud: 'God, if you are real, come and give me peace.'

I wasn't expecting much, but something really did happen that night. A presence entered my cell – a warmth that quickly turned into more. The waves of unrest started to settle, the fears began to disappear and for a moment, I felt like I was a child being held in the arms of a parent. The peace came quickly and in such an unlikely place. I knew that this wasn't just in my head. It was the God of heaven himself, sending his Spirit to bring me tranquillity, comfort and peace.

That night I slept – I really slept. And I woke up knowing that I had encountered the peace of God in my prison cell.

Today, I visit prisons in my role as the international director of 24-7 Prayer in Great Britain. 24-7 Prayer helps prisoners to encounter God in prayer – and we believe that these God-encounters can bring life transformation.

Brian Heasley is the International Prayer Director for 24-7 Prayer in Great Britain. You can read more of Brian's story in his book *Gatecrashing* (Edinburgh: Muddy Pearl, 2014). Story supplied by 24-7 Prayer. Used with permission.

 MARK 6:6-13

'Jesus went around teaching from village to village. He called the 12 disciples to him. Then he began to send them out two by two. He gave them authority to drive out evil spirits.

Here is what he told them to do. "Take only a walking stick for your trip. Do not take bread or a bag. Take no money in your belts. Wear sandals. But do not take extra clothes. When you are invited into a house, stay there until you leave town. Some places may not welcome you or listen to you. If they don't, leave that place and shake the dust off your feet. That will be a witness against the people living there."

They went out. And they preached that people should turn away from their sins. They drove out many demons. They poured olive oil on many sick people and healed them.'

SOMETHING TO THINK ABOUT

Jesus sent his disciples out in pairs. That way they could encourage each other. But they were not to rely on their own strength or preparation. Instead, they went with a simple message, doing what they had seen Jesus do. What can we learn and put into practice in our lives today?

Prayer

Heavenly Father, I want to be someone who helps other people to know Jesus. Show me how. Amen.

'You will call out to me for help.
And I will answer you.
You will cry out.
And I will say, "Here I am."'
ISAIAH 58:9

'Sometimes I think, "I won't talk about his message anymore.
I'll never speak in his name again."
But then your message burns in my heart.
It's like a fire deep inside my bones.
I'm tired of holding it in.
In fact, I can't.'
JEREMIAH 20:9

15 New work to do

I was brought up in Moss Side in quite a dysfunctional family. My parents split up when I was very young, and for many years I was physically abused by my mum, who was an alcoholic.

When I reached my early teens I turned to hard-core raving at the Haçienda in Manchester to try to escape the pain. I went from being addicted to ecstasy, to addicted to alcohol. Later, when I was married with three children, the drink still had a hold on me and I lost my husband and my kids.

I did get my life back on track for a while when I graduated from Manchester University with a degree in criminology in 2008. But after having another child, my life went out of control again.

I ended up in an alcohol-dependent relationship, which led to me going to HMP Styal for a wounding offence. I was really in a dark place. I was very angry, confused and lost.

Rest for the weary

But all that began to change when I met the prison chaplain. I asked her if she could pray for the victim of my offence and his family, as well as my own family, which she did. Then she offered me a New Testament, which I took upstairs to my room. The first scripture I turned to was from Matthew 11 – 'Come to me all who are weary...'

– and I thought, 'That's me.' So I said to God, 'If you're real, prove it – because I want to rest. I'm tired of this.' That night I said sorry for everything I'd done and asked God to forgive me if he loved me. Then I went to sleep.

The next morning, I felt really calm. When I spoke to the chaplain she encouraged me to continue to read my New Testament. After that I kept going to chapel, wanting to know so much more. I had so many questions about how to have this peace and freedom, so I joined the Bible study group. The chaplains broke it down for me.

Change noticed

For the first eight weeks I was in a single cell and I absolutely devoured the New Testament. I stopped swearing and smoking. My whole attitude totally changed. It was unbelievable because I was so angry when I first got there. I was growling at everyone. I wasn't a very nice person. I was always on the defensive, very judgmental and just wanted to lock myself away from everybody.

But now I didn't want to be seen as this violent, angry woman. I had been holding on to a lot of hurt and fear. I realised I could give it all to God, and I thought, 'This is amazing – I am actually loved.' It just completely changed me. I'd been broken, but God was rebuilding me. I knew this was part of his plan for me because there was no other way he could've gotten through to me.

Officers noticed such a change in me that they moved me to an open unit in the prison. Then they asked me if I would like to work at the Message Enterprise Centre (MEC). The chaplain explained it was a café, and they do a lot of work with ex-offenders. I was flabbergasted. For someone to put their trust in me gave me such a sense of hope.

Restored

When I was released from prison I was amazed when I was offered a full-time job at the MEC. I'm still in shock, really! There are people working here who are going through what I've been through, and I have been able to support them and tell them that they can pray and ask God for help.

My life wouldn't be where it is now if it wasn't for The Message Trust. It's not just a job that they've given me. They've given me self-worth, and I feel so valued as a team member. I'm just so grateful that they've given me this opportunity to show that I'm not just another statistic or another offender.

God has now restored my family life back to even better than it's ever been. My daughter is stunned that she's got a mum. When I left she was eight. She's 18 now and we've got a really good relationship. She trusts me again.

This is God, and I thank him every day.

Contributed by an ex-offender.

 MARK 6:39–44

'Then Jesus directed them to have all the people sit down in groups on the green grass. So they sat down in groups of 100s and 50s. Jesus took the five loaves and the two fish. He looked up to heaven and gave thanks. He broke the loaves

into pieces. Then he gave them to his disciples to pass around to the people. He also divided the two fish among them all. All of them ate and were satisfied. The disciples picked up 12 baskets of broken pieces of bread and fish. The number of men who had eaten was 5,000.'

SOMETHING TO THINK ABOUT

In this story, Jesus took the little that the people had and he did something amazing! What could he do with what you bring to him?

Prayer

Heavenly Father, I am amazed that you want to involve me in your rescue plan for this troubled world. Please show me what you want me to do. Amen.

'Take my life and let it be
Consecrated, Lord, to Thee.
Take my moments and my days,
Let them flow in endless praise.'
FRANCES RIDLEY HAVERGAL (1836–1879)

'God loves us deeply. He is full of mercy.'
EPHESIANS 2:4

16 Saved

My life of crime started at age eight, when I began stealing. By the time I was ten, I had a real taste for money. I was hanging out with the wrong crowd and getting into a lot of fights. Aged 16, I got into a particularly bad fight and got very badly beaten up. That day, gangsters took me in and brought me up.

I served my first prison sentence when I was 17 – but to me this was not a deterrent but a badge of honour. A lot of my friends had been in prison and I was proud to be there. The next time I went into prison I started to realise that I'd let my family down, and I felt a sense of remorse – but because I'd had a taste for money, I continued to get in trouble with the law.

By the age of 18 I'd had my first child. I didn't know how to be a father to my daughter as my own dad left me when I was young. I also started to dabble with cocaine at this time. I needed money to fund this drug-use, so my life spiralled out of control. I also became very abusive.

Empty

I had the opportunity to go to college on a business studies diploma, but I kept getting into trouble. After becoming threatening at college, I was kicked out and sent back to prison.

I was in and out of prison for the next 15 years, and being introduced to crack cocaine during this time changed my life completely. After one particularly heavy four-day binge, I remember coming home to an empty house. It was a cloudy day and, as I looked at the black clouds, I sat there thinking, 'I've done it again.' I screamed at the top of my voice, 'Is anyone there?' and the black clouds cleared and light came on my face – I knew someone was listening and there was hope.

But my drug addiction continued to spin out of control. On one occasion, after overdosing, I collapsed and my friend tried to revive me – but it was ten minutes before I was responsive. He thought I had died.

Change witnessed

Shortly after that, at Christmas 1999, I met up with two old friends who had also been caught up with drugs and crime, but they had turned their lives around. I saw the change in them and I knew I wanted what they had. They told me that it was Jesus who had changed their lives, and that they had found out about him at a Christian rehab centre.

I was definitely interested, but after that Christmas, I returned to crack cocaine. I had experienced a traumatic event in which five guys threatened me with guns while I had my daughter with me. That triggered a nervous breakdown. I wanted to kill the person who had pulled the gun on me.

In February 2000, a friend from Ireland told me firmly that I needed to change my life as I was destroying my family. I could go to a rehab to turn my life around. I remember saying to God, 'If you can do for me what you did for my friends, then do it for me.'

Future hope

I went into rehab, and haven't looked back since – and that was 17 years ago. I got clean and returned to London, where I began working in social care and developing a successful career.

I thought I was going to die a drug addict, in prison, or in a psychiatric unit, because that was the way my life was heading – until someone told me about Jesus Christ, who changed my life. I'm now celebrating ten years of marriage, I'm pastor to a thriving church, and I've been invited to preach and teach in prisons. God has given me hope and a new future.

Contributed by an ex-offender.

 MARK 6:45–51

'*Right away Jesus made his disciples get into the boat. He had them go on ahead of him to Bethsaida. Then he sent the crowd away. After leaving them, he went up on a mountainside to pray.*

Later that night, the boat was in the middle of the Sea of Galilee. Jesus was alone on land. He saw the disciples pulling hard on the oars. The wind was blowing against them. Shortly before dawn, he went out to them. He walked on the lake. When he was about to pass by them, they saw him walking on the lake. They thought he was a ghost, so they cried out. They all saw him and were terrified.

Right away Jesus said to them, "Be brave! It is I. Don't be afraid." Then he climbed into the boat with them. The wind died down. And they were completely amazed.'

SOMETHING TO THINK ABOUT

Sometimes Jesus does things that are humanly impossible. The disciples were surprised to see Jesus walking on the lake. But they should have known he would help them. Are there times in life when you need to hear Jesus say: 'Be brave! It is I. Don't be afraid'?

Prayer

Dear God, 'I do believe! Help me overcome my unbelief!' (Mark 9:24). Amen.

'Perfect love drives away fear...
fear has to do with being punished.'
1 JOHN 4:18

'God, you are the one who saves us.
We will trust in you.
Then we won't be afraid.
LORD you are the one who gives us strength.
You are the one who keeps us safe.
LORD, you have saved us.'
ISAIAH 12:2

Week 3 – Identity revealed

Love is at the heart of the Jesus story. In Mark 9:7, God's voice from heaven is heard saying: 'This is my Son, and I love him. Listen to him!' These words are similar to the words heard at Jesus' baptism (Mark 1:11).

In John 3:16 we read: 'God so loved the world that he gave his one and only Son. Anyone who believes in him will not die but will have eternal life.' God sent Jesus to show us his love.

Jesus also promises to love us. He said, 'Anyone who has my commands and obeys them loves me. My Father will love the one who loves me. I too will love them. And I will show myself to them' (John 14:21). We show our love for God by following Jesus and living God's way, instead of living to please ourselves.

Jesus is revealed as the 'Messiah' – the Saviour the Jewish people had been expecting. They were expecting a conquering king who would save them from Roman rule, just like Moses had led them out of captivity in Egypt. Jesus surprised them. He wasn't what they expected.

As you read the Bible passages and prison stories this next week, think about how God shows his love to people. How does God show his love and care to you, and to others through you?

READ: MARK CHAPTERS 7–9

Key verses

'Jesus and his disciples went on to the villages around Caesarea Philippi. On the way he asked them, "Who do people say I am?"

They replied, "Some say John the Baptist. Others say Elijah. Still others say one of the prophets."

"But what about you?" he asked. "Who do you say I am?"

Peter answered, "You are the Messiah."'

Mark 8:27-29

THINK

1. Jesus asked his disciples, "Who do you say I am?" When asked, some people today say Jesus was just a good man, or a prophet. What would you say if he asked you the same question?

2. In the past week we have read several stories about Jesus' miracles. Which story stands out most from your perspective and why?

3. In Mark chapters 7–9 we read about Jesus healing people. Notice how every healing is different. Jesus doesn't use a formula – he treats each person as an individual. What are the differences in the healing stories you have read this week?

4. What do you think Jesus meant when he said, 'Whoever wants to be my disciple must say no to themselves. They must pick up their cross and follow me' (Mark 8:34)? The Bible passage quoted in the prison story on Day 19 helps to explain: 'Take your everyday, ordinary life—your sleeping, eating, going-to-work, and walking-around life—and place it before God as an offering' (Romans 12:1, *The Message*).

5. In Mark 9:24 we read about a father who came to ask Jesus to heal his son. He wanted to believe Jesus could help and said, 'I do believe! Help me overcome my unbelief!' Do you find it difficult to believe that Jesus is God's Son? What evidence and experience do you have to share with others?

LIFE LESSONS

1. God speaks to each of us in different ways. This week we read about Abdul who had a dream (Day 11). How does God speak to you?

2. Which of the prison stories you have read this week stands out most for you and why?

3. How has God answered your prayers recently?

4. In the Old Testament book of Jeremiah, God makes a promise:

> '"I know the plans I have for you," announces the
> LORD. "I want you to enjoy success. I do not plan to
> harm you. I will give you hope for the years to come.
> Then you will call out to me. You will come and pray
> to me. And I will listen to you. When you look for me
> with all your heart, you will find me. I will be found
> by you," announces the LORD.' (Jeremiah 29:11–14).

Many people in prison and out of prison find encouragement from these verses. It is as if God is speaking these words today to each of us personally. How do you respond to this promise?

LOOK AHEAD

In the coming week we will see that Jesus makes enemies of many of the rich and powerful people in Jerusalem. For many of the people he met face to face, it was decision time: would they follow him or not?

As we follow the story of Mark's Gospel, Jesus is heading to Jerusalem and his execution. There are surprises along the way in how he reacts. See who the important people are in Jesus' opinion. Find out what Jesus' top priority is in living God's way.

17 Changed on the inside

From a young age, Shane started to burgle houses and steal cars. He stabbed people and sold drugs. Soon he was on the run for kidnapping and attempted murder.

Shane eventually got caught and was put in prison, but his incarceration did little to stem his rebellion. His hatred of authority saw him stab two prison officers after he wasn't allowed to use the prison gym. It sparked a riot.

His out-of-control behaviour quickly saw him transferred to a high security prison. Even then he needed further locking up, and was placed within a close supervision system.

'They felt I was a danger to everybody,' Shane says. 'They had to feed me through a hatch in the door because they couldn't have physical contact with me.'

He's real!

Then Shane met Robert, who had been imprisoned for murder, but had since become a Christian. 'He was saying a load of things that sounded mad to me,' says Shane, 'but the one thing that stuck in my mind was when he said, "I've been in prison for 15 years and am probably never getting out – but I'm free." I used to think, "What's he on about?"'

Shane felt an urge to start writing to Robert, and began reading the Bible that was in his cell. He was then moved to another prison, where a minister invited him to an Alpha course.

'I said, "Yeah, put my name down." I was mostly interested in getting the chocolate biscuits and having debates.'

It was about halfway through doing Alpha that Shane experienced the presence of God for the first time. 'I said, "Jesus, I know you died on a cross for me. I don't like who I am... please forgive me." I started to feel tears coming into my eyes. I tried to hold it back. But it rose up, until suddenly I began crying my eyes out. I hadn't cried in years. I cried for about five minutes, and I could feel a weight being lifted off me,' Shane remembers. 'In that split second I knew it was real. I knew God existed, I knew Jesus had touched me and that I was going to live for him forever.'

Amazing love

Shane's behaviour changed so much that within weeks he went from being in permanent segregation to getting a trusted job in the prison chaplaincy. He no longer saw the prison officers as the enemy.

'Not long after all this, I was lying on my bed in my cell. All the bad things I'd done to people flicked through my head and all the times I'd upset people – and I started crying. It occurred to me that for many years I'd been aggressive towards people without even realising it.'

Almost exactly a year after the Alpha day, Shane was freed from prison. He started going to church where, seven months later, he met his future wife, Sam.

The couple got married in church in October 2008, with 100 family and friends celebrating with them.

'Jesus has changed my life,' Shane says. 'Jesus has shown me how to love and how to forgive. Almost all the people I've upset, all the people I stabbed, all the people I hurt, have forgiven me and now we talk – it's amazing.'

Story contributed by Alpha. Used with permission.

MARK 7:14–16,21–23

'*Again Jesus called the crowd to him. He said, "Listen to me, everyone. Understand this. Nothing outside of a person can make them 'unclean' by going into them. It is what comes out of them that makes them 'unclean'.*

Evil thoughts come from the inside, from a person's heart. So do sexual sins, stealing and murder. Adultery, greed, hate and cheating come from a person's heart too. So do desires that are not pure, and wanting what belongs to others. And so do telling lies about others and being proud and being foolish. All these evil things come from inside a person and make them 'unclean.'"'

SOMETHING TO THINK ABOUT

Someone once wrote to the Christian Enquiry Agency asking what meat Christians can eat. Jesus' words in today's reading are good news for meat-eaters! It's what we *do* that puts a barrier between us and God, not what we eat. The good news is, Jesus' death on the cross destroyed the barrier. If we ask, Jesus can forgive all the wrong we've ever done and make us clean.

Prayer

This prayer was written by the Jewish King David after he had committed adultery with Bathsheba, then arranged for Bathsheba's husband to be killed:
'Wash me, then I will be whiter than snow.
Let me hear you say, "Your sins are forgiven."
That will bring me joy and gladness.
Let the body you have broken be glad.
Take away all my sins.
Wipe away all the evil things I've done.' (Psalm 51:7-9)
Amen.

'"Come. Let us settle this matter,"
says the LORD.
"Even though your sins are bright red,
they will be as white as snow.
Even though they are deep red,
they will be white like wool.'

ISAIAH 1:18

18 Deep needs met

As a child, what I wanted most was to be safe – but I was abused. I remember being locked in my bedroom and being woken up in the early hours of the morning by drunk people. I used to hear my mum being beaten up and hear my sister crying. I was hungry a lot of the time. I went into care when I was seven.

I carried [the abuse] around with me. By the time I was 12 or 13 I had a strong dislike for men. I would attack men at will because I hated them, and I hated myself for what they did to me as a child.

At 14 I went into youth custody and by 16 was suffering from mental illness. My life was such a mess – I tried to kill myself twice. I was abusing my life with drugs, and became addicted to heroin. I saw psychologists and psychiatrists, but I kept going back to my past.

Second chance

One judge told me to stop being a victim and become a survivor. That changed my life. I realised that I couldn't change the things that happened to me as a child, but I could change my future.

I was finally diagnosed with schizophrenia about nine years ago. I was in a mental health hospital, and they said I could stay for as long as I wanted. I looked around and saw lots of old men. I didn't want that for my future. That's when I realised I needed to fight to get out, and I did. I was also put on the right medication, which helped so much.

A Christian rehabilitation charity gave me a second chance. I was able to grow as a person, and the staff were so supportive. It was OK to say to staff that I was having a bad day, and they would say, 'Come and have a coffee.' An act of generosity or kindness, no matter how small, makes a massive difference. My support worker believed in me – he never judged me. That made a huge difference on my road to recovery. If people don't believe in you, you struggle to believe in yourself.

Important job

For the first time, I'm part of a community and settled. I now advise police and trainee mental health students on how to treat people with mental health issues in custody. I feel brilliant when I'm doing it – like an important cog in the machine. I can get away with saying things that psychologists and probation officers can't! Last year, I came second for 'service user of the year' in an NHS award. That's probably been my proudest moment. I get up on cold mornings because it's worth it. I want to reach hundreds of people. I want everyone to have positive experiences while they're in custody if they've got mental health issues.

I embrace my life now. The last nine years have been the best years of my life – I've finally got a life! I enjoy what I do. If I can help one person it's been worthwhile. My advice is to never give up. You might get it wrong every now and then, but never give up.

Contributed by Langley House Trust. Used with permission.

MARK 7:31–35

'Then Jesus left the area of Tyre and went through Sidon. He went down to the Sea of Galilee and into the area known as the Ten Cities. There some people brought a man to Jesus. The man was deaf and could hardly speak. They begged Jesus to place his hand on the man.

Jesus took the man to one side, away from the crowd. He put his fingers into the man's ears. Then he spit and touched the man's tongue. Jesus looked up to heaven. With a deep sigh, he said to the man, "Ephphatha!" That means "Be opened!" The man's ears were opened. His tongue was freed up, and he began to speak clearly.'

SOMETHING TO THINK ABOUT

Throughout the Gospels, we read about Jesus making a difference to people's lives. He treated each person as an individual. He didn't follow a formula when he healed people. He knew their deepest needs. He took this man away from the crowds and, at his command, the man's deaf ears were opened and he could hear. Today's testimony shows how God can use Jesus' followers to help others. God cares for each of us individually and wants to meet our deepest needs.

Prayer

Heavenly Father, I am so glad that you know me and love me anyway. Help me to accept other people and to show them what Jesus is like. Amen.

'Cleanse me from my sin, Lord,
put Thy power within, Lord,
take me as I am, Lord,
and make me all Thine own.'

R. HUDSON POPE (1879–1967)

'Constant kindness can accomplish much. As the sun makes ice melt, kindness causes misunderstanding, mistrust, and hostility to evaporate.'

ALBERT SCHWEITZER (1875–1965)

19 An invitation

My defining experience growing up was my dad walking out of the family home when I was six. I remember it as plain as day, even 40 years later. It seemed to set my future direction, because I spent all my early years in the shadow of that event. I craved attention and would get it wherever I could. Sport became an early means of getting that attention and medicating my low self-esteem, but as I moved into my teens, sport was replaced by sex and drugs to try to block out the pain of my dad's rejection.

By the age of 18 I had dropped out of school and moved to Southern Spain. Free from any home restraints, I became heavily involved in the drug scene. The following year I returned to the UK only to be arrested and charged as part of a Europe-wide drugs cartel. At just 20, I found myself the youngest in the dock alongside seasoned criminals who were facing charges for drug trafficking, extortion and murder.

Invited to hope

After serving time in three different prisons I was released, and I tried to put my life back together. Despite my best efforts to redefine myself, I could not shake the feelings of despair and hopelessness.

One evening, when I was feeling particularly low, I found myself walking into a small village church. It was there that I heard an invitation full of hope: 'Come to me, all you who are tired and are carrying heavy loads. I will give you rest' (Matthew 11:28). It was an invitation to go on a journey with Jesus; a journey that would be full of uncertainties but also full of hope and freedom, and ultimately the certainty of eternal life.

Despite the fact that I was surrounded by a room full of strangers, I accepted that invitation. I knew God was speaking to me directly. The desire to be free from the trap I found myself in was far greater than my fear of looking foolish and crying out for help.

Peace

I cried for the first time since my father walked out. I felt overwhelmed by the love of God. Every new tide of tears brought a release of pain, anger and fear. That fear was replaced by a peace I had never experienced before. The following day, I found a Bible and read these words:

'So here's what I want you to do, God helping you: Take your everyday, ordinary life—your sleeping, eating, going-to-work, and walking-around life—and place it before God as an offering. Embracing what God does for you is the best thing you can do for him. Don't become so well-adjusted to your culture that you fit into it without even thinking. Instead, fix your attention on God. You'll be changed from the inside out. Readily recognize what he wants from you, and quickly respond to it. Unlike the culture around you, always dragging you down to its level of immaturity, God brings the best out of you, develops well-formed maturity in you' (Romans 12:1–2, *The Message*).

From that point on I knew, no matter how difficult it might be, that God had broken into my life. He had washed away the pain and the guilt and redefined my future. I no longer needed to seek approval and medicate the pain. God had revealed the full extent of his Father heart of love for me and I knew peace for the very first time.

God's good plans

Slowly I began to grow as a Christian. The transformation I had read about began to take place, impacting my relationships and affecting every part of my life. God gave me a family and allowed me to prosper in business.

I have found that God, our heavenly Father, is not a liar. When he says he has a plan for our lives – plans to give us a hope and a future – he means it (see Jeremiah 29:11). That is not to say it is going to be easy. It's a challenging journey. It was for me and it is for anyone who is serious about following Jesus. But it is worth it.

Contributed by an ex-offender.

MARK 8:27–29

'Jesus and his disciples went on to the villages around Caesarea Philippi. On the way he asked them, "Who do people say I am?"

They replied, "Some say John the Baptist. Others say Elijah. Still others say one of the prophets."

"But what about you?" he asked. "Who do you say I am?"

Peter answered, "You are the Messiah."'

SOMETHING TO THINK ABOUT

Many of the people Jesus met were expecting a 'Messiah' – a king who would rescue them from Roman rule. Even the disciples didn't expect this Messiah to die a criminal's death nailed to a Roman cross. No one expected Jesus to change the world by defeating the biggest enemy of all: death. Jesus turns lives around in surprising ways. How is Jesus working in your life?

Prayer

Dear God, please take control of my life. Please show me how to use each moment. Let my life cause people to praise you. Amen.

'Here is how God has shown his love for us. While we were still sinners, Christ died for us.'

ROMANS 5:8

20   A second chance

I was born in Larne, Northern Ireland, which is about 20 miles from Belfast. I am the elder of two, and was brought up in a very staunch Protestant home. We were an ordinary working class family and went to church out of tradition.

I left school at 15 with no qualifications and got a job in a local furniture shop. I decided that when I was old enough, I would join the Army. So I signed up for six years and saw service in Africa, Germany and England.

I lost a number of friends who served in Northern Ireland. In 1972 it came to our door when my dad's cousin was kidnapped and murdered by the IRA. I was getting ready to return to civilian life and was home on leave when this happened. I insisted that I wanted to attend the funeral, which the Army wasn't happy about. It was a paramilitary funeral in Loyalist Belfast. I went back to my regiment still very angry about this brutal murder.

Interrogated

I left the Army in early 1973 and, shortly afterwards, was asked about joining the UDA, the Ulster Defence Association, the largest Protestant paramilitary group. I saw that as an opportunity to get revenge, so I joined and was involved in acts of terrorism in the East Antrim area.

Although I was never in doubt that my past would catch up with me, I tried to continue to live as normal a life as possible. I got married and started a family.

In the early hours of one September morning in 1980, I was arrested under the Prevention of Terrorism Act and interrogated for seven days. At the end, I was broken, especially mentally. I had been charged with murder and was remanded in custody to Crumlin Road Prison in Belfast. It was during that long remand period that I thought about my life. I wanted a second chance if possible. So, one night in my prison cell, I asked God to help me and give me that second chance. He answered my prayers.

H-block

In 1982 I came to trial and was charged with murder amongst other offences. Halfway through, the murder charge was dropped to manslaughter – a real answer to the prayers of my Christian friends. I pleaded guilty.

I received 12 years for manslaughter and was sentenced in total to 152 years in prison on 52 counts under the Prevention of Terrorism Act to run concurrently. I went to the H-Block of the Maze Prison. There I met men who had given their lives to Christ: murderers, a bomber, a fellow terrorist, and many more who had come to know Christ. As a result, they had had their lives turned round for the better; Loyalists as well as Republicans.

Sensing the Lord's presence in my cell one day, I fell on my knees and said, 'What do you want me to do while I'm in prison, Lord?'

A thought came to me after I'd prayed: 'Billy, I want you to use this time to study, to educate yourself, and to prepare yourself for full-time Christian service after your release from prison.' I could hardly believe my ears. Despite my initial scepticism, I shrugged and said, 'At least it's a clear answer to my question!'

A new chapter

Billy was released in 1987. After going to Bible College, he worked for Prison Fellowship Northern Ireland, then moved to Switzerland where he volunteered with Prison Fellowship Switzerland before returning to the UK in 2001.

Today Billy is based in Doncaster, where he works amongst society's broken people. He says: 'It is very challenging, but rewarding because it was in the darkness that I found hope and most importantly freedom as Jesus set me free. Looking back over all these years, I realise God gave me that second chance – and a full pardon.

You can find out more by reading Billy McFetridge and Michael Apichella, *Full Pardon* (Milton Keynes: Malcolm Down Publishing, 2015).

Story adapted from *Inspire* magazine. See www.inspiremagazine.org.uk

 MARK 8:34–36

'Jesus called the crowd to him along with his disciples. He said, "Whoever wants to be my disciple must say no to themselves. They must pick up their cross and follow me. Whoever wants to save their life will lose it. But whoever loses their life for me and for the good news will save it. What good is it if someone gains the whole world but loses their soul?"'

SOMETHING TO THINK ABOUT

Jesus invites us to be part of his upside-down kingdom. As Francis of Assisi is believed to have said in the 12th century, 'It is in giving that we receive, it is in pardoning that we are pardoned, and it is in dying that we are born to eternal life.' God is no man's debtor. Test him out. Give him all of your life. Then watch how he responds with overflowing love.

Prayer

Father God, thank you for loving me and for sending Jesus to live, die and rise again so I can know your love. I am so grateful. Please use me to share your love with others. Amen.

'God, create a pure heart in me.
Give me a new spirit that is faithful to you.'
PSALM 51:10

'Love so amazing, so divine,
Demands my soul, my life, my all.'
ISAAC WATTS (1674–1748)

21 Transformed

John Lawson was born in Glasgow in 1966. His parents moved to South Africa in 1969, where his father was a law enforcement officer. His brother Alex was born in 1972 and all seemed like happy families.

But four years later, after a family trauma, John's parents split up. His father remained in South Africa, but John, Alex and their mother moved back to Drumchapel, Scotland, which had a reputation as the roughest housing estate in Europe. That's where John learned to use violence to resolve a situation.

Later, John moved to Merseyside where he developed an interest and skill for martial arts. He started work as a bouncer and then moved into bodyguard work, getting involved with a highly professional group of ex-soldiers from various countries who became an elite team. Their employer would use them to clean up troubled nightclubs, in which the motto was, 'hit them hard and move on'.

Bad decisions

John said of this period of his life, 'I kinda always felt I had the moral high ground – I think I watched too many John Wayne movies when I was a kid. I made a lot of stupid decisions because of that mentality.'

Working with big bands like The Rolling Stones, REM, and AC/DC gave John the desire for the high life. He was soon involved in kidnapping men that had stolen from some of his clients. Embroiled in a world of shotguns, kidnapping and money, he made a lot of cash. Money was his god.

Subsequently, John ended up in prison serving a five-year sentence for extortion. His wife left him. His home was sold, and all his worldly possessions were confiscated by the state. But he didn't care. He figured he would do another job when he got released, and be back on top.

However, one night in February 2005, the persistence of a Nigerian friend in prison led John to the Christian Fellowship in Saughton Prison, Edinburgh. Initially he was reluctant, until he found out the meetings were stocked with sugary treats! He admitted: 'I thought Christians were weak, vulnerable, pathetic people. I planned to fill my pockets as soon as they were all praying with their eyes closed.'

Intrigued

John met with God that night. As other hardened criminals sang gospel songs, he wept like a baby behind the song sheet. He woke the next day in his cell with an amazing sense of peace.

The story of Jesus at the well with the Samaritan woman (John 4:1–42) intrigued him. As he read, he felt God's presence in his cell. The following week, he headed back to the Christian Fellowship group meeting. The combination of his mother's prayers, the prison pastor and, most importantly, the grace of God, led him to turn away from his old life and surrender to Jesus.

Now, John has realised that the greatest place he could ever have gone to was prison! He says: 'Prison can take many forms – you don't need to be locked up, to be in a prison.' There are no walls that can ever hold John again for he is 'free' indeed!

Read John's story in John Lawson and John Sealey, *If A Wicked Man* (Sutton Coldfield: RP Publishing, 2016). Used with permission.

 MARK 9:2-8

'After six days Jesus took Peter, James and John with him. He led them up a high mountain. They were all alone. There in front of them his appearance was changed. His clothes became so white they shone. They were whiter than anyone in the world could bleach them. Elijah and Moses appeared in front of Jesus and his disciples. The two of them were talking with Jesus.

Peter said to Jesus, "Rabbi, it is good for us to be here. Let us put up three shelters. One will be for you, one for Moses, and one for Elijah." Peter didn't really know what to say, because they were so afraid.

Then a cloud appeared and covered them. A voice came from the cloud. It said, "This is my Son, and I love him. Listen to him!"

They looked around. Suddenly they no longer saw anyone with them except Jesus.'

SOMETHING TO THINK ABOUT

God meets with people in unexpected places. Jesus and his closest friends were climbing a mountain when Jesus was revealed to them in a new way. Back in Jewish history, Moses had given them God's laws. Elijah was the most famous of Israel's prophets. Jesus is identified as purer and greater than all who had come before him. Once again, God describes Jesus as his much-loved Son. Jesus makes it possible for us to enter God's presence. Where do you meet with God?

Prayer

Thank you, Jesus, for opening up the way for me to know God. Help me to point the way for others to know him too. Amen.

'LORD, you will give perfect peace to those who commit themselves to be faithful to you.'

ISAIAH 26:3

22   A reconciled child

Having been a prison chaplain for 15 years, there are some events that I will never forget. I met Steve* when he arrived at the prison. The last person he wanted to see was the chaplain. He had grown up in a stable home with lovely Christian parents. His dad had worked for a period as a prison governor, so ending up inside had never been part of Steve's life plan.

Through various events, Steve had become estranged from his parents and his life had spiralled downwards. At a particular low point he had a heated argument with a troublesome neighbour, which ended in Steve assaulting him. As a result, Steve was arrested and later imprisoned.

Running away from God, Steve ended up working in the prison as the chapel orderly. Over a period of time his faith was rekindled and he recommitted his life to Jesus. But he was still estranged from his parents, who had been very hurt by choices he had made.

Saying sorry

Working with probation officers, we reached out to Steve's parents and arranged a family meeting as part of the resettlement strategy. I was in the room with Steve, his mum and his dad, and two other prison staff. It was a major step for Steve to be able to say 'sorry', followed by a long embrace with his mum, who unashamedly cried her eyes out saying, 'Thank you so much, I have got my son back.'

Incredibly, I knew the pastor of the church where Steve's mum and dad were members. With Steve's permission, I contacted the pastor and arranged for him to visit Steve in the prison. On release, Steve – now in his thirties – returned home for about a year, living with his parents again, where he could be supported by them and the pastor of their church.

About a year after Steve left the prison, his dad contacted me to simply say that things were going well. Steve had left home again, but was in regular contact with them. He was enjoying his work and continuing to grow in his Christian faith.

*Names have been changed. Contributed by a prison chaplain.

MARK 9:33-37

'Jesus and his disciples came to a house in Capernaum. There he asked them, "What were you arguing about on the road?" But they kept quiet. On the way, they had argued about which one of them was the most important person.

Jesus sat down and called for the 12 disciples to come to him. Then he said, "Anyone who wants to be first must be the very last. They must be the servant of everyone."

Jesus took a little child and had the child stand among them. Then he took the child in his arms. He said to them, "Anyone who welcomes one of these little children in my name welcomes me. And anyone who welcomes me also welcomes the one who sent me."'

LUKE 15:11-24

'Jesus continued,

"There was a man who had two sons. The younger son spoke to his father. He said, 'Father, give me my share of the family property.' So the father divided his property between his two sons.

"Not long after that, the younger son packed up all he had. Then he left for a country far away. There he wasted his money on wild living. He spent everything he had. Then the whole country ran low on food. So the son didn't have what he needed. He went to work for someone who lived in that country. That person sent the son to the fields to feed the pigs. The son wanted to fill his stomach with the food the pigs were eating. But no one gave him anything.

"Then he began to think clearly again. He said, 'How many of my father's hired servants have more than enough food! But here I am dying from hunger! I will get up and go back to my father. I will say to him, "Father, I have sinned against heaven. And I have sinned against you. I am no longer fit to be called your son. Make me like one of your hired servants."' So he got up and went to his father.

"While the son was still a long way off, his father saw him. He was filled with tender love for his son. He ran to him. He threw his arms around him and kissed him.

"The son said to him, 'Father, I have sinned against heaven and against you. I am no longer fit to be called your son.'

"But the father said to his servants, 'Quick! Bring the best robe and put it on him. Put a ring on his finger and sandals on his feet. Bring the fattest calf and kill it. Let's have a feast

*and celebrate. This son of mine was dead. And now he is alive
again. He was lost. And now he is found.' So they began to
celebrate."'*

SOMETHING TO THINK ABOUT

In God's topsy-turvy kingdom, God gives priority to the
poor, the weak and the vulnerable. Status, riches and
knowledge don't impress him. As Philip Yancey said in
What's So Amazing About Grace?: 'Grace means there is
nothing we can do to make God love us more... And grace
means there is nothing we can do to make God love us
less—no amount of racism or pride or pornography or
adultery or even murder. Grace means that God already
loves us as much as an infinite God can possibly love.'**
Jesus waits with open arms to welcome us into God's family.

**Philip Yancey, *What's So Amazing About Grace?* (Grand Rapids, MI, USA: Zondervan, 1997)

Prayer

Thank you, Father God, for loving me. Amen.

Week 4 – Decision time

At this point in our journey with Jesus, the ending is revealed. The 12 disciples know that Jerusalem is a dangerous place for Jesus. They know that he has made enemies, and there are plots to kill him. They are afraid, but Jesus is determined. He knows what to expect. Talking about himself as the 'Son of Man', he says:

> 'The Son of Man will be handed over to the chief priests and the teachers of the law. They will sentence him to death. Then they will hand him over to the Gentiles. They will make fun of him and spit on him. They will whip him and kill him. Three days later he will rise from the dead!' (Mark 10:33–35)

Jesus' followers had a lot to learn. They found these words difficult to believe until they found themselves face to face with the risen Jesus, with the wounds in his hands and feet still visible from the crucifixion.

They still expected a king to overthrow the occupying Roman army. They wanted short term benefits. They couldn't grasp that Jesus was starting a new kingdom that would go on forever. They didn't understand that in Jesus' kingdom there are very different priorities. People who expect to be last, like children and poor people, are those who are first in God's kingdom (Mark 10:44). No wonder Jesus made enemies of the rich and powerful people!

READ: MARK CHAPTERS 10–12:40

Key verses

'Jesus called them together. He said, "You know about those who are rulers of the Gentiles. They hold power over their people. Their high officials order them around. Don't be like that. Instead, anyone who wants to be important among you must be your servant. And anyone who wants to be first must be the slave of everyone. Even the Son of Man did not come to be served. Instead, he came to serve others. He came to give his life as the price for setting many people free."'
Mark 10:42-45

THINK

1. Looking at the Bible readings in Mark's Gospel last week and this week, what surprises you about the pecking order in Jesus' kingdom? Who is first and who is last?

2. Jesus saw that the rich young man (Day 23) loved money more than he loved God. What do people put first in their lives? What about you? What's the most important thing in your life?

3. As Jesus entered Jerusalem, the crowds welcomed him as a hero. Days later, another crowd was calling for him to be crucified. How do the people you know respond to Jesus?

4. One of the men who came to Jesus with a question realised that to 'love God with all your heart and mind and strength is very important. So is loving your neighbor as you love yourself' (Mark 12:33). What examples can you give of people living this way?

5. Does it surprise you that Jesus drove the traders out of the temple courtyard? When is it right to be angry? How should we act when we are angry?

LIFE LESSONS

1. Pariti Emmanuel's story (Day 23) shows how significant it can be to forgive and to be forgiven. Are there people you need to contact to forgive or to be forgiven?

2. Jesus gives blind Bartimaeus his sight (Mark 10:46–52). Stephen, who told his story on Day 24, began to explore who Jesus is by reading the Bible. He changed from being someone who was spiritually blind to a man who could see who Jesus is. Where are you on the journey from being spiritually blind to seeing?

3. When Daz (Day 25) was sent to prison he used his time to study the Bible. He found support from the people in his fiancée's church. Do you know of churches who support people in prison, or ex-prisoners? How can you link with these churches or help make a link between your church and your local prison?

4. Jim (Day 26) has found that it is possible to be in prison and to feel free inside. Have you found the freedom Jesus gives? What difference does it make to your life?

LOOK AHEAD

In the next week we will discover that actions speak louder than words. What we do shows what we believe. Ask God to help you understand yourself better as you take special notice of the way you act towards God and towards the people around you.

23 Following Jesus

Pariti Emmanuel participated in the 1994 Genocide against the Tutsis. 'I murdered many Tutsis under the order of bad leadership,' he said.

Emmanuel grew up a Hutu, in a village in the Eastern Province of Rwanda. Rwanda had seen many years of conflict and unrest leading up to the 1994 Genocide due to divisions between the Hutu and Tutsi people groups. However, on 7 April 1994, a 100-day-long mass killing led to the death of more than 800,000 Tutsis, leaving the country in chaos.

After the Genocide ended in July 1994, Emmanuel was arrested and sent to prison where he spent the next six years, before the start of the Gacaca courts – a Rwandan community justice system that worked towards restoring the nation.

Reconciliation

For Rwanda to be able to move forward as a country, it became important for its people to be reconciled – to be able to live together in peace. Prisoners were encouraged to tell the truth about what they had done for the sake of closure and reconciliation. Emmanuel explained, 'I spoke the truth during the Gacaca courts and was sentenced to ten years in prison.' But because he was willing to tell the truth, and because he had already spent six years in prison, he was allowed to serve the remaining four years in community service.

During his time in prison, fellow prisoners invited Emmanuel to an Alpha course. Seeing something different in these prisoners, he went. But although he felt encouraged by Alpha at the time, he struggled to cope with the things he had done, and found he wasn't able to fully engage. Emmanuel felt he needed to be forgiven for what he had done. 'I wrote a letter asking for forgiveness from the people whose relatives I murdered… and I found peace in my heart.'

Family problems

Despite this peace, Emmanuel's experiences outside prison proved to be equally difficult. 'When I came back to the community, I found my wife with two children that were not mine. I kept wondering how I would live with the Genocide survivors. To me, that was a big problem. I never liked meeting a survivor. Whenever I met one I would hide. That shows the state of my heart back then. My heart was filled with agony, loneliness and fear.'

Remembering the encouragement he had found doing Alpha in prison, Emmanuel decided to contact the chaplain who had run his Alpha course, and he did Alpha again. 'I learned that Jesus forgives, and experienced love in a way I had never known before. [I realised] I needed to forgive my wife, like I had been forgiven even though I had murdered people. I forgave my wife and took care of the children.'

Meeting victims

Having experienced a profound sense of freedom and peace in his new-found relationship with God, and being reconciled with his wife, Emmanuel decided he wanted to ask for forgiveness from the relatives of his victims in person. With the help of his pastor – formerly his chaplain – Emmanuel went to find Vincent, whose mother and grandmother he had killed.

Vincent explained that it wasn't easy seeing Emmanuel coming to ask for forgiveness after what he had put his family through during the Genocide. However, he felt it was important to extend forgiveness to Emmanuel. 'For the sake of unity and reconciliation, I told Pariti not to be embarrassed to meet me. It wasn't easy to say such words to someone like Pariti, who had committed such atrocities. But I realised that with God, everything is possible, so I decided to forgive.'

Today, Emmanuel and Vincent live in the same village. They have formed a friendship, and now, Emmanuel says, 'I no longer feel the shame and embarrassment I felt before. I understand that Jesus forgives and, I have peace in my heart. I have found healing and forgiveness for the things that I have done.'

Contributed by Alpha. Used with permission.

MARK 10:17-22

'As Jesus started on his way, a man ran up to him. He fell on his knees before Jesus. "Good teacher," he said, "what must I do to receive eternal life?"

"Why do you call me good?" Jesus answered. "No one is good except God. You know what the commandments say. 'Do not murder. Do not commit adultery. Do not steal. Do not be a false witness. Do not cheat. Honor your father and mother.'"

"Teacher," he said, "I have obeyed all those commandments since I was a boy."

Jesus looked at him and loved him. "You are missing one thing," he said. "Go and sell everything you have. Give the money to those who are poor. You will have treasure in heaven. Then come and follow me."

The man's face fell. He went away sad, because he was very rich.'

SOMETHING TO THINK ABOUT

Jesus puts his finger on what comes between us and God. For the rich young man, it was his love of money. For Pariti Emmanuel in today's story, it was his lack of forgiveness. Is there anything in your life that comes between you and God?

Prayer

Father in heaven, thank you for loving me. Help me to put you first in my life, today and always. Amen.

24 A reward

When a group of ex-prisoners walked into Stephen James' prison and began sharing their stories of change, healing, and forgiveness, Stephen didn't think he'd ever be one of them.

'I went up to the guy who was running the ministry and said, "You don't know how bad I've been." I started to list every bad thing I'd done in my life when he stopped me. He told me, "I don't want to know about what you've done. We love you, and Jesus loves you."'

That day was a turning point for Stephen who, at 25 years old, was serving a four-year sentence in HMP Shrewsbury, England, for drug possession.

Stephen was the youngest of five children. His father was an alcoholic, and his mother withered under his father's physical and psychological abuse.

'There wasn't any love,' says Stephen. 'No encouragement, no investment in the children. We grew up in fear.'

Downward spiral

Stephen often questioned the bad things that happened in his life. His school performance suffered, and at 15 years old he began to follow in his father's footsteps, working in construction by day, and drinking his nights away.

'I lived my life in the bars, pubs, and clubs,' says Stephen. 'And that progressed to drugs.' It started with cannabis, and quickly spiralled into speed, ecstasy, and LSD. 'Then I was introduced to methadone, which is a substitute for heroin addicts. But to get it, you have to show up to the doctor with heroin in your system, so you can claim you were an addict.'

But it wasn't just a claim. 'I started dealing. The low point of my life was using intravenously – injecting five to six times a day. I was suicidal and remember thinking I couldn't carry on like this.'

In 1995, Stephen was caught and convicted for possession of heroin, and sentenced to four years in prison. He served two. At that point, he was convinced he would go back to drugs when he was released. But transformation was already taking shape, as Stephen began asking the 'God' question.

'If you'd have asked me if there is a God, I would have said yes. But I didn't know him personally.'

Near the end of Stephen's sentence, men from a Christian rehabilitation charity visited his prison. They brought ex-offenders with them, who shared their stories of brokenness, drug addiction, and alcohol abuse. This got Stephen's attention.

Abandoned

'I identified with them,' he says. 'I'll never forget when I was in prison: I was abandoned. My family didn't want to know me. Nobody visited me. I didn't think my life could change. But they all said that Jesus changed their life. And that was the moment for me.'

Stephen opened a Bible and began his exploration of who Jesus is, why he came, and what he wanted Stephen to do. He found the answers to his questions about life, and purpose, and identity. Stephen committed his life to Jesus.

When Stephen was released from prison in August of 1997 he was determined not to go back. He moved to South Wales, where a rehab charity supported his reintegration for two years, while he rebuilt his life. He worked in construction while he went back to school, eventually earning a college degree in sociology and social studies. He met his wife, got married, and started a family.

Back to prison

Then, in 2008, a group from Christianity Explored Ministries approached Stephen to develop a course based on the Gospel of Mark, to be taught in prisons.

'I didn't want to go back to prison,' says Stephen. 'But I felt a calling to go back. It was clear that God wanted me to be involved in prison ministry.' Stephen spent the next eight years developing and teaching what would become the basis for Prison Fellowship International's programme, 'The Prisoner's Journey'.

Stephen regularly watches men and women come into the course saying the same things he used to say – 'I can't change, you don't know where I've been' – and sees them, step-by-step, begin to understand and live the message and hope of Jesus.

'One of the most rewarding things I've heard a prisoner say is, "I'm more free in prison than I would be outside, now that I have Christ in my life."'

Contributed by Lindsey A. Frederick at Prison Fellowship International. Used with permission.

MARK 10:46-52

'A blind man was sitting by the side of the road begging. His name was Bartimaeus. Bartimaeus means Son of Timaeus. He heard that Jesus of Nazareth was passing by. So he began to shout, "Jesus! Son of David! Have mercy on me!"

Many people commanded him to stop. They told him to be quiet. But he shouted even louder, "Son of David! Have mercy on me!"

Jesus stopped and said, "Call for him."

So they called out to the blind man, "Cheer up! Get up on your feet! Jesus is calling for you." He threw his coat to one side. Then he jumped to his feet and came to Jesus.

"What do you want me to do for you?" Jesus asked him.

The blind man said, "Rabbi, I want to be able to see."

"Go," said Jesus. "Your faith has healed you." Right away he could see.'

SOMETHING TO THINK ABOUT

Jesus made it possible for Bartimaeus to see, and he also healed the spiritual blindness of the man in today's prison story. Are there areas where you are blind to the truth? Ask Jesus today to speak to you about what is true and what is false.

Prayer

Faithful Father, thank you for hearing me when I talk to you. Help me to hear what you are saying to me. Amen.

25 Incredible!

Daz became fascinated with violence from a young age. When his uncle took him to see a Millwall versus Manchester City football match, Daz remembers seeing fans ripping up seats and throwing them into the stands of rival supporters. Even though Daz was just a kid, he was gripped by these images, and years later he became a violent football thug himself. He thought that if people feared him he would have respect – something he craved.

When he decided that he needed to start carrying a knife, he bought five Stanley knives for him and his friends to take to a Millwall match. During a fight between rival fans, he used his knife to slash someone's face. On the train back to London, Daz and his friends were hyped up and buzzing as they talked about the violence they'd committed. But after a while the mood changed and it went quiet. Daz suddenly felt a sense of emptiness.

A date with God

When he began dating the girl who is now his wife, she started asking him to go to church. That really baffled him. He didn't believe in God, and thought that if God did exist, 'Why would he want to know a scumbag like me?' The only dealings Daz had had with a church before was when he stole the DJ equipment that they used for the youth club.

But his girlfriend kept asking him to come to church, and persuaded him to attend an Alpha course where he could learn the basics about Christianity and ask questions. Daz had told her, 'If I do the Alpha course, and I find out that there's no God, I don't ever want you to mention God to me again, and I will never ever come to church with you again.'

While the Alpha course was running, Daz continued to get into trouble. One night he stabbed someone and was charged with GBH. He was due to appear at Woolwich Crown Court at a later date.

Incredible force

By the end of the Alpha course, he still didn't believe in God but was asked if he wanted prayer to receive the Holy Spirit. Very reluctantly he went forward for prayer, and wasn't really listening to what was prayed for him. He was just about to open his eyes and turn around to his girlfriend to say, 'That's it. I told you it was a load of rubbish. God is not real...' when, all of a sudden, he felt this incredible force surging through his body. It was overpowering. It was exactly what he had needed. He had felt the presence of God in an unmistakable and powerful way.

For the next two weeks Daz felt like his life was transformed. He stopped carrying a knife and he felt an overwhelming sense of love. He no longer felt that something was missing in his life, and he felt like God had filled the emptiness in his heart.

Found guilty

But his past caught up with him. In 2007, Daz appeared at the Old Bailey and was found guilty of manslaughter on the grounds of diminished responsibility. He was subsequently locked up for four years. He was 19 years old.

In prison, he was blown away by the amount of support he received from people at his now-fiancée's church. He had a lot of time to study the Bible and think about God.

He was released in 2011, and in the summer of 2012 he married his fiancée. Their son was born in January 2014.

If you met Daz today, you would find it hard to believe that he was once a violent killer. He is tall and slim with cropped dark hair. He speaks articulately with a strong Cockney accent. And one of the first things you notice about him is that he has a calm and gentle spirit. Daz says, 'If God can change me he can change anyone. He has helped me rebuild my life, and I have a love in my heart that is indescribable.'

Daz's story is contributed by Paul Warwick. Used with permission. See www.paul-warwick.co.uk

MARK 11:1–2,7–10

'Jesus sent out two of his disciples. He said to them, "Go to the village ahead of you. Just as you enter it, you will find a donkey's colt tied there. No one has ever ridden it. Untie it and bring it here..."

They brought the colt to Jesus. They threw their coats over it. Then he sat on it. Many people spread their coats on

*the road. Others spread branches they had cut in the fields.
Those in front and those in back shouted,*

"Hosanna!"

"Blessed is the one who comes in the name of the Lord!"

"Blessed is the coming kingdom of our father David!"

"Hosanna in the highest heaven!"'

SOMETHING TO THINK ABOUT

Jesus arrived in Jerusalem as Jews were arriving from
all over the known world for the Passover celebrations.
Passover reminded them how they had been set free
from slavery in Egypt. Now they were living under
Roman occupation and wanted a king to set them free.
Jesus, riding on a donkey's colt, wasn't what they were
expecting, but they welcomed him like a conquering king.
In Daz's story, God wasn't what he expected either. What
surprises you about Jesus when you read about him?

Prayer

God of surprises, I want to know you. Amen.

'My grace is all you need. My power is
strongest when you are weak.'

2 CORINTHIANS 12:9

26 A changed man

Jim Cavanagh spent over 20 years in federal prisons across Canada. He grew up in a dysfunctional home and would get progressively angry witnessing his alcoholic dad abuse his mother.

'I started stealing, and the stealing soon led to armed robberies,' Jim says.

His first 15 years in prison, Jim continued to become increasingly violent. He was hurting, withdrawn, anti-social, and he started to hate himself because he saw himself as a failure.

'I hurt a lot of people in bad ways,' Jim says. 'If someone had done something wrong to me and I felt justified, I would go after that person with a vengeance because I had so much hatred within me. My fellow prisoners learned that if they had a problem with me, either they needed to kill me, or I would kill them.'

No remorse

Jim became so hardened, he says he didn't feel remorse.

He was introduced to Jesus by another prisoner who went through a conversion while in prison. This man was an ex-bank robber, and Jim had a lot of respect for him.

Jim says, 'If someone other than my own friend [told me about Jesus], I would have told them to get lost. But since it was my friend, who I knew wouldn't lie to me, and I had seen the change in his life, I knew there had to be something there that was real. He wasn't leading his old style of life. But it wasn't until I reached out in prayer that God met me right where I was at in that prison cell. And I started my walk of faith with the Lord.'

Free inside

Other inmates at first thought Jim's change was a game being played – that it wasn't real. 'Yet they saw the change that was taking place over the months and years, and how I walked away from the violence. And this spoke to them,' says Jim.

Jim continues, 'It was an inner-healing I received and I felt free inside. I didn't have to try and escape anymore, I was already free. I was able to forgive myself, and have love and appreciation for myself. And then God enabled me to love my fellow prisoners and have forgiveness toward them whenever they would do something to offend me. God is bringing about an internal change, and with that internal change is external evidence.'

You can read Jim Cavanagh's story in his book *Captured: To Run No More* (Ontario: Ernie Hollands Hebron Ministries Inc., 2012). Contributed by Leilani Squires at Prison Fellowship International. Used with permission.

MARK 11:15–19

'When Jesus reached Jerusalem, he entered the temple courtyard. He began to drive out those who were buying and selling there. He turned over the tables of the people who were exchanging money. He also turned over the benches of those who were selling doves. He would not allow

anyone to carry items for sale through the temple courtyard. Then he taught them. He told them, "It is written that the Lord said, 'My house will be called a house where people from all nations can pray.' But you have made it a 'den for robbers.'"

The chief priests and the teachers of the law heard about this. They began looking for a way to kill Jesus. They were afraid of him, because the whole crowd was amazed at his teaching.

When evening came, Jesus and his disciples left the city.'

SOMETHING TO THINK ABOUT

As thousands of people arrived in Jerusalem to celebrate Passover, the money changers and merchants saw an opportunity to make a profit. Their stalls were set up in the temple's courtyard so worshippers could change money into the temple currency and buy animals for the ritual sacrifices. Jesus was angry. The temple was a place for people to pray, but the traders made it a place of extortion. The money changers and merchants were becoming wealthy at the expense of worshippers. Jesus took action. Being angry isn't wrong when it's anger against injustice. But it is important that we know how to direct our anger and control it. Jesus' righteous anger provoked the religious leaders. He threatened their authority, so they began plotting to have him killed.

Prayer

Heavenly Father, teach me to be angry about the things that anger you. Help me to know how to act when I'm angry. Make the fruit of your Holy Spirit grow in my life, especially self-control, when I am angry. Amen.

'May the mind of Christ my Saviour
Live in me from day to day
By His love and power controlling
All I do and say'

KATE WILKINSON (1859-1928)

'The fruit the Holy Spirit produces is love, joy and peace. It is being patient, kind and good. It is being faithful and gentle and having control of oneself. There is no law against things of that kind.'

GALATIANS 5:22-23

27 Lost faith

At the age of 21, I came to know Jesus. It was 7 February, my birthday. For five years I did seaside mission work, and it was at one of these events that I met my wife, Patricia. We got married in 1971 and I moved from Glasgow to Sunderland, Patricia's hometown. I had a good job, and at that time I felt that I had been richly blessed by God. To make it more of a blessing, we were going to have our first child in July 1973. Sadly, it was a stillborn girl, and deep sorrow filled our home for the loss of our daughter, who we named Rebeka.

But I lost more than just my child. I lost my faith in God. I could not believe that God would allow this to happen to us. So for a long time, we wept and just about gave up hope – but God had not given up on us.

Grieving

Almost two years later my wife had become pregnant again, but didn't tell me until late in her pregnancy – mainly because we were still grieving and full of uncertainty. But in October 1975, our first son was born, and a few years later in December 1979, our second son was born.

You would think I would have been happy, but no – I was still far away from God. I walked in a kind of wilderness for years and, as a result of doing what I wanted to do, I ended up in prison, a complete wreck –

no wife, no children, no faith, no God. Yet God still loved me even in there.

One day, while at work in the laundry at Manchester Prison, I saw a young man reading a Bible. I was compelled to talk with him. I also went to a Bible class with him, and that is when I came back to God and faith in him.

God's promise

God used a woman called Kath to pray for me in 2008. When she did, I was filled with the Holy Spirit and given the text: 'For I know the plans I have for you... plans to prosper you and not to harm you, plans to give you hope and a future' (Jeremiah 29:11, NIV).

The Lord has been true to his word. I have been healed of a 'cup hand', and have been used by the Lord in many ways. I am praying that the Lord will grant me Cat D at some point, but in the meantime, I continue to study his Word and pray with my fellow brothers and sisters in the Lord.

Contributed by a prisoner.

MARK 12:13-17

'Later the religious leaders sent some of the Pharisees and Herodians to Jesus. They wanted to trap him with his own words. They came to him and said, "Teacher, we know that you are a man of honor. You don't let other people tell you what to do or say. You don't care how important they are. But you teach the way of God truthfully. Is it right to pay the royal tax to Caesar or not? Should we pay or shouldn't we?"

But Jesus knew what they were trying to do. So he asked, "Why are you trying to trap me? Bring me a silver coin. Let me look at it." They brought the coin. He asked them, "Whose picture is this? And whose words?"

"Caesar's," they replied.

Then Jesus said to them, "Give back to Caesar what belongs to Caesar. And give back to God what belongs to God."

They were amazed at him.'

SOMETHING TO THINK ABOUT

The Pharisees and Herodians were two rival groups in Jerusalem when Jesus was there. But they were united in their dislike of Jesus. The Pharisees were religious leaders. They enforced rules about how to live. Jesus described them as white-washed tombs: 'How terrible for you, teachers of the law and Pharisees! You pretenders! You are like tombs that are painted white. They look beautiful on the outside. But on the inside they are full of the bones of the dead' (Matthew 23:27).

The Herodians supported a ruler who had been ousted by the Romans. Their power had already been undermined.

Both groups tried to trap Jesus with their tax question. If Jesus said, 'Yes, pay Caesar's tax', he would have angered the people. 'No' would have triggered harsh state penalties.

Jesus' wise answer defused the situation. No matter how hard they tried to provoke him, Jesus did nothing wrong.

Prayer

Father in heaven, thank you for loving me. Teach me to be wise when people try to provoke me. When bad things happen, help me to trust you. Help me to follow Jesus today and every day. Amen.

'If any of you needs wisdom, you should ask God for it. He will give it to you.'

JAMES 1:5

'No one can serve two masters at the same time. You will hate one of them and love the other. Or you will be faithful to one and dislike the other. You can't serve God and money at the same time.'

MATTHEW 6:24

28 What's missing?

In 2014, I was three-and-a-half years into a life sentence with a minimum term of ten years. Although I had got over the shock of it all a long time ago, and I was reasonably happy getting by, I felt I had something really missing in my life – something I could not explain.

A lot of my friends at the time were Christians, and they said what I was missing was Jesus. I instantly set about trying to make a mockery of their statements and this apparent man who was 2,000 years old and had died but lived again. I thought it was hilarious, but as time went by, I found myself doing things I could not explain – like wanting to listen to a Christian radio station, or reading the Bible. I finally put my pride to one side and I prayed to God that, if he was real, would he show himself to me.

Fears gone

Soon enough, all my anxieties and fears were gone. Physically, I was incarcerated in a prison with two massive cage like fences keeping me in, but mentally I was free and protected like Daniel when he was in the den with the lions (Daniel 6). On 19 December 2014, I accepted Jesus into my life as my Saviour.

My life has changed so much for the better. Every day, the Lord shows himself to me with blessings and an abundance of hope. I know now he has a path for my future. Last year, Jesus showed me favour on my retrial, and my life sentence was changed to a normal sentence. I was also so blessed to be baptised in the place I accepted Jesus into my heart.

Mercy found

I take hope from Paul's words in 1 Timothy 1:12–14: 'I am thankful to Christ Jesus our Lord. He has given me strength. I thank him that he considered me faithful. I thank him for appointing me to serve him. I used to speak evil things against Jesus. I tried to hurt his followers. I really pushed them around. But God showed me mercy anyway. I did those things without knowing any better. I wasn't a believer. Our Lord poured out more and more of his grace on me. Along with it came faith and love from Christ Jesus.'

With Jesus in our life, God will shower us with love, faith, and most importantly hope and forgiveness. For our God is a forgiving God and, even though it took me a while to get over the shame of my former sinful self, he has helped me through every step of the way and helped me to become a better person. I make mistakes daily, but with the Lord's forgiveness I am able to become the man I want to be.

Contributed by a prisoner.

MARK 12:28-33

'One of the teachers of the law came and... asked him, "Which is the most important of all the commandments?"

Jesus answered, "Here is the most important one. Moses said, 'Israel, listen to me. The Lord is our God. The Lord is one. Love the Lord your God with all your heart and with all your soul. Love him with all your mind and with all your strength.' And here is the second one. 'Love your neighbor as you love yourself.' There is no commandment more important than these."

"You have spoken well, teacher," the man replied. "You are right in saying that God is one. There is no other God but him. To love God with all your heart and mind and strength is very important. So is loving your neighbor as you love yourself. These things are more important than all burnt offerings and sacrifices.'"

DANIEL 6:26-27

'I order people in every part of my kingdom to respect and honor Daniel's God.

He is the living God.

He will live forever.

His kingdom will not be destroyed.

His rule will never end.

He sets people free and saves them.

He does miraculous signs and wonders.

He does them in the heavens and on the earth.

He has saved Daniel

from the power of the lions.'

SOMETHING TO THINK ABOUT

There were hundreds of religious laws in Jesus' time. But Jesus summarised them all into two simple statements. When we love God, we want to live to please him. Jesus offers a relationship, not a rule book.

Jesus said, 'If you love me, obey my commands. I will ask the Father. And he will give you another friend to help you and to be with you forever' (John 14:15–16). That 'friend' is his Holy Spirit. As we follow Jesus we are changed. Our actions towards others show God's love to them too.

Prayer

Heavenly Father, help me to love you with my whole heart. Amen.

'But God is faithful and fair. If we confess our sins, he will forgive our sins. He will forgive every wrong thing we have done. He will make us pure.'

1 JOHN 1:9

Week 5 – Actions speak

Jesus knew what he was letting himself in for when he went to Jerusalem. He knew that many religious people would reject him. Some wanted him dead. He had the power to stop them, but he chose not to. His motive was love for people like us. He didn't just talk about being loving, he showed his love through his actions.

READ: MARK CHAPTERS 12:41–14:52

Key verses

'While they were eating, Jesus took bread. He gave thanks and broke it. He handed it to his disciples and said, "Take it. This is my body."

Then he took a cup. He gave thanks and handed it to them. All of them drank from it.

"This is my blood of the covenant," he said to them. "It is poured out for many. What I'm about to tell you is true. I won't drink wine with you again until the day I drink it in God's kingdom."'

Mark 14:22-25

THINK

1. Jesus saw the heart of the widow who gave everything she had (Mark 12:41–44). He also knew the motives of Judas when he complained about money being spent on an expensive jar of perfume (Mark 14:3–8). God does

not look at outward appearances. He looks at our heart attitudes. How are people judged in today's world? How should Jesus' followers act differently?

2. As well as looking forward to his own death and resurrection, Jesus looked forward to the end of time (Mark 13). Jesus has promised to return (John 14:1-3). How can we live in the light of that promise?

3. Jesus used a meal to explain how he would die. His body would be broken, and his blood spilt. He knew that his followers would go on breaking bread and pouring wine at meals, so they would be able to remember what he had done. Have you shared this special meal? It can be called Communion, Mass, the Eucharist or the Lord's Supper. What does this meal mean to you?

4. Jesus' closest friends deserted him when he needed them most. He knows what it is like to be abandoned. How does this make you feel?

LIFE LESSONS

1. 'God, if you're out there... help me.' That was Ashley's prayer from prison (Day 30). God hears our prayers, even when we aren't sure who we are praying to. God answered Ashley's prayer and has turned his life around. How has your life changed since you got to know about Jesus?

2. In Steve's story (Day 31), he was amazed by the kindness of strangers; people from a local church who he might never meet. Those people received no reward. But God saw their hearts. What motivates you? Do you live to please yourself or to please God?

3. Brian (Day 33) was in Dartmoor Prison when he asked God to change him. He now works with people who are in prison, just like he was. 'A lot of my work is with people who have failed,' he says. Jesus said, 'I have not come to get those who think they are right with God to follow me. I have come to get sinners to follow me' (Mark 2:17). How does that make you feel?

4. The prison story on Day 34 reminds us that God promises that when we search for him we will find him (Matthew 7:7–8). That can happen in a prison cell or a palace. Getting to know God through his Son Jesus is the journey of a lifetime. Where are you on the journey?

LOOK AHEAD

Jesus didn't just say kind words or talk about loving people. He showed his love by dying on a cross to make it possible for us to experience God's love for ourselves. This is the mystery at the heart of our Christian faith. God does not demand that we reach up to him. He doesn't expect us to pay our way into his presence. Instead, he became a human being and lived among ordinary people, people like us who let him down. If we ask him, he forgives all our shortcomings and gives us his power to make a fresh start in life. He promises to be with us always, guiding us and supporting us, whatever life throws at us.

In the coming week, we will reach the end of the first part of the Jesus story. The second part continues in lives changed through history and today. Is your story part of the worldwide Jesus story?

29 Giving everything to God

Still in a somewhat dazed state, the clunk of the cell door behind me brought me to my senses and I realised that life as I had known it had changed forever. Gone was the respect of my family and friends, my affluent middle-class lifestyle and, of course, my freedom.

As I took in my new accommodation, the last moments of sunlight filtered into the small room, highlighting the plumes of cigarette smoke emanating from the lower bunk. As a non-smoker, I found this very unpleasant, but figured my objections would not be a good way to introduce myself to my cellmate. So we just exchanged the usual pleasantries and I made up my bunk before settling in for the night.

Doom and despair

The first few days on induction were really tedious. I felt a growing sense of doom and despair welling up inside me. I was eventually moved to a main residential wing where, naively, I had expected better accommodation – but the only change was that the smell of cigarettes had been replaced by the smell of urine.

For the first time in my life I felt totally helpless and alone, and my frustrations were beginning to turn into unfamiliar feelings of anger within me; a literal ticking time bomb. I was scared. These feelings were alien to me and I had no one to turn to. Although I considered myself to be an atheist, I found myself praying to God for help, but of course I figured my sorry mumblings were in vain and thought nothing more of it.

Chatty chaplain

A couple of days later I was sitting alone in my cell, aware of a dark presence in the shadows of my mind, when the cell door opened and a smiling face looked in. He enquired after my cellmate. My tone must have conveyed a sense of despair as he introduced himself as a prison chaplain, and asked if I would like to have a chat. I figured, 'Why not?'

He sat and chatted with me for half an hour, and for the first time since coming into prison, I felt a sense of calm. I thanked him for his time and, before he left, he gave me a book to read. It was the story of a lady who had a very serious illness, but as a practising Christian had unwavering faith in God's willingness to help her deal with her troubles. I couldn't believe how someone could have such faith in God while suffering such adversity. I realised that God was with me too. He listens to and answers my prayers. Since then, he has taken me on an amazing spiritual journey to a place of peace, joy and contentment, which I could never have imagined. He has shown me the way to a new sense of hope for a bright and prosperous future.

Contributed by a prisoner.

MARK 12:41-44

'Jesus sat down across from the place where people put their temple offerings. He watched the crowd putting their money into the offering boxes. Many rich people threw large amounts into them. But a poor widow came and put in two very small copper coins. They were worth only a few pennies.

Jesus asked his disciples to come to him. He said, "What I'm about to tell you is true. That poor widow has put more into the offering box than all the others. They all gave a lot because they are rich. But she gave even though she is poor. She put in everything she had. That was all she had to live on."'

SOMETHING TO THINK ABOUT

Jesus often talked to his followers about money. This story shows he notices the poor and the weak. He is not impressed by wealth and status. He looks for followers who are whole-hearted in loving God and generous-hearted with their possessions. God is more concerned about the attitude of our hearts than the amount of money in our pockets. Whatever our background or position in life, Jesus wants to show us how much God loves us.

Prayer

Father in heaven, you see my heart attitude.
Please help me to put you first in my life.
I want to follow Jesus wholeheartedly. Amen.

'Lord, make me an instrument of your peace:
where there is hatred, let me sow love;
where there is injury, pardon;
where there is doubt, faith;
where there is despair, hope;
where there is darkness, light;
where there is sadness, joy.'
FRANCIS OF ASSISI (1181-1226)

'True Christians consider themselves
not as satisfying some rigorous creditor,
but as discharging a debt of gratitude.'
WILLIAM WILBERFORCE (1759-1833)

'LORD, have mercy on us.
We long for you to help us.
Make us strong every morning.
Save us when we're in trouble.'
ISAIAH 33:2

30   The return

I had always been a troublemaker for as long as I can remember – by the time I was 13 I was getting into trouble with the police.

I was taking drugs. I'd been arrested for shoplifting. I'd done burglary, arson, criminal damage. There was something about getting into trouble that really excited me. The more I tried to sort myself out, the worse I got.

I was selling most drugs in nightclubs. Those places that I wasn't selling drugs, I made sure I had people selling drugs for me. I started to get noticed by people above me. It wasn't long before I was selling drugs for them. We were buying drugs from people like the Albanian mafia and we were selling to the likes of Hell's Angels. I was looking for fulfillment in drugs, in sex, in power, in my status. The only problem is that when you have a status – a reputation – you have to live up to that. You've got to do things to make sure people don't take that from you.

Armed

The guy that I was selling drugs for phoned me up and told me he'd been attacked by a rival gang. He asked me to go to one of the safe houses and pick up a firearm. I was nervous about what was going to happen. But I went to the safe house and put on a brave front. I picked up a firearm, and I remember leaving the house with the intention to kill. If we'd have found the people we were looking for, I'd have pulled the trigger. Thankfully I never had to do what I thought I was going to have to do. At that point I realised that I desperately needed help.

But I couldn't help myself. As I got into more and more trouble, I ended up in prison, suddenly realising – 'You're not a gangster. You're an idiot. You've messed up your life. Now you've got to deal with the consequences. You're in prison.'

In danger

A prisoner who'd been transferred with me started to talk to me about God. I couldn't understand what I was hearing. Here I was in prison with my life in danger, and this guy wanted to talk to me about God. How could God help me in the situation I'd got myself into?

It was a couple of days later that I was walking past the chapel sign-up sheet, and I signed up. For some reason, at that very moment, a sense of peace hit me that I'd never experienced anywhere else before. I remember going back to my cell and saying something along the lines of, 'God, if you're out there, if you are who these people say you are, then help me. Whatever I have to do, whatever the cost to me, I am yours. I give my life to you. Please take my life and do with it whatever you want.'

The gang that I was involved with were caught in a drugs raid and taken off the streets. The relationships I was in started to break down. This gave me more and more time to work on my relationship with God.

God's power

I was no longer a drug addict. There was no drugs rehabilitation. No counselling. No replacement therapy. It was just the power of God, his Word and prayer.

What I found when I went to church was something different. People were different. They seemed to have a sense of joy about them. They were loving and caring, and they just accepted me for who I was.

I'm looking forward to the future. I'm not entirely sure where this journey is going to lead me, but I'm looking forward to seeing where it's going. My life has changed massively. I'm working with a local youth group trying to encourage them not to make the same mistakes that I made.

Ashley told his story to yesheis UK. Used with permission.
The video of Ashley telling his own story is available at
www.greatcommission.co.uk/ashleys-story-from-yesheis

 MARK 13:5–8,26

Jesus said to them, "Keep watch! Be careful that no one fools you. Many will come in my name. They will claim, 'I am he.' They will fool many people. You will hear about wars. You will also hear people talking about future wars. Don't be alarmed. These things must happen. But the end still isn't here. Nation will fight against nation. Kingdom will fight against kingdom. There will be earthquakes in many places. People will go

hungry. All these things are the beginning of birth pains... people will see the Son of Man coming in clouds. He will come with great power and glory.'

SOMETHING TO THINK ABOUT

God promises that one day there will be an end to poverty and suffering. We need to be wary of false teachers claiming to be God's special messengers. Jesus will return and it will be unmistakable. Until then we can focus on developing our relationship with God, and putting his words into practice as we show his love to those we meet.

Prayer

Dear Jesus, I look forward to your return. Please help me to stay close to you today and every day. Amen.

'"[God] will wipe away every tear from their eyes. There will be no more death." And there will be no more sadness. There will be no more crying or pain.'

REVELATION 21:4

31 Kindness

When I was released from prison, some members of the church met me at the gates and took me to the house. No one had ever done that for me before and it made me feel a bit less anxious. I felt like someone actually cared about what happened to me.

We arrived at the Hope into Action house and I was told that it would be my home. The house itself was so lovely. It was clean and had everything I would need. People from the church had pitched in to help furnish the house, so I had a bed to sleep on, a sofa to sit on and a table to eat at. I was surprised that people who I'd never met had obviously put in so much effort to make it feel homely for me.

That first night, I had a welcome meeting with Steve, the vicar of the local church. We had a meal together, cooked by one of the volunteers at the house. For the first time in as long as I could remember, I felt welcome and wanted.

Support

Steve talked through everything with me and reassured me that the people from Hope into Action would help support me getting back into employment. We also went through lots of other housekeeping things together like paying bills, so that I knew exactly what needed to be paid and when. He said it might take a while for my benefits to arrive, so they gave me some foodbank vouchers to get me through in the meantime.

I met my housemate the day I moved in. It felt a bit strange to suddenly be sharing a house with a complete stranger, but in some ways, I liked the fact that I wasn't on my own. He'd been there a while, so he seemed very much at home and said he'd show me the ropes over the next few days. I was pleased there was someone who I could ask where the nearest bus stop was and the local shop.

Privacy and peace

It was an amazing feeling to have my own room for the first time in ages. Just the privacy of not having to share a bedroom felt really good. It was really peaceful – I hadn't realised how much the noise of the prison bothered me until I noticed the peace and quiet of the Hope into Action home.

Having a bathroom felt like a bit of a luxury after sharing facilities with loads of other blokes in prison. Someone had thoughtfully provided some clean towels and toiletries for me to use.

Wanted and welcomed

It's hard to describe how I felt the first night I slept in the house; I think it was a mixture of anxiety and excitement. Here I was, in my new home, living with someone I'd only met an hour or so before. Everything was different.

The weirdest thing was that a bunch of complete strangers from a church I'd never been to had worked so hard to make me feel wanted and welcomed. They actually seemed to care what happened to me. I wasn't used to feeling like that. It was strange... but I really felt touched by it.

Contributed by Hope into Action. Used with permission.

MARK 14:3–8

'Jesus was in Bethany. He was at the table in the home of Simon, who had a skin disease. A woman came with a special sealed jar. It contained very expensive perfume made out of pure nard. She broke the jar open and poured the perfume on Jesus' head.

Some of the people there became angry. They said to one another, "Why waste this perfume? It could have been sold for more than a year's pay. The money could have been given to poor people." So they found fault with the woman.

"Leave her alone," Jesus said. "Why are you bothering her? She has done a beautiful thing to me. You will always have poor people with you. You can help them any time you want to. But you will not always have me. She did what she could. She poured perfume on my body to prepare me to be buried."'

SOMETHING TO THINK ABOUT

Just as Jesus acknowledged the poor widow who gave all she had (page 152; Mark 12:41–44), he also gave credit to this woman who poured valuable perfume on his head. This same story is told by John, one of Jesus' closest friends and an eyewitness to the events in Jesus' life.

In his Gospel he explains that Judas Iscariot objected to the extravagance of this woman's gift because he was in charge of the money bag and used to help himself to what was in it. He didn't care about poor people (John 12:4-6).

God looks at our hearts. He sees what motivates us. He wants Jesus' followers to have the same generous, loving heart as he has. Our actions should speak as loudly as our words about God's love.

Prayer

Dear God, help me to show others what your kingdom is like; help me to be more like Jesus. Amen.

'Christians should work harder toward establishing colonies of the kingdom that point to our true home... If the world shames a social outcast, the church will proclaim God's reconciling love... That, at least, is the vision of the church in the New Testament: a colony of heaven in a hostile world.'
PHILIP YANCEY*

*Philip Yancey, *What's So Amazing About Grace?* (Grand Rapids, MI, USA: Zondervan, 1997)

32 Fresh start

At 26, John* had spent three terms in prison, offences including robbery and importing drugs. After his second term he had a real desire to reform for the sake of his daughter, but found that his old associates pulled him back into crime.

On his third sentence he decided to keep his head down and use prison as a positive experience, studying and using training opportunities. An avid reader, he worked his way through the Koran, the Torah and the Bible. Attracted to the God of the Bible, he began to see that there could be hope for his future, and he worked all the more to give himself as strong an advantage as possible.

Volunteering

Upon leaving prison, John spent some months in a hostel, and some in a tent in a local country park. During this time he was contacted by User Voice, a charity that enables ex-offenders to support one another, and he started volunteering regularly for them. He was referred to Hope into Action for supported accommodation, and was given a place in one of their houses. With the combined support of User Voice and Hope into Action, John has begun to realise his dream of being able to support his daughter, having been offered paid work with User Voice.

During his time with Hope into Action, John was invited to speak at the Hope into Action annual conference alongside former MP Jonathan Aitken and Paul Cowley OBE. John spoke about his time in prison, explaining how he had met God there, which gave him hope and enabled him to use his time positively. He had an amazing impact on those who heard him as he shared how God had spoken to him through Psalm 25:6-7:

> 'Remember your mercy, O LORD, and your steadfast love,
> for they have been from of old.
> Remember not the sins of my youth or my transgressions;
> according to your steadfast love remember me,
> for the sake of your goodness, O LORD!' (ESV)

John still struggles with managing his money, and has some unhelpful friends and associates who would like to drag him down. But by majoring on his strengths rather than his weaknesses, Hope into Action is working with him to help him realise his dreams.

*Names have been changed.

Contributed by Hope into Action. Used with permission.

MARK 14:17-24

'When evening came, Jesus arrived with the 12 disciples. While they were at the table eating, Jesus said, "What I'm about to tell you is true. One of you who is eating with me will hand me over to my enemies."

The disciples became sad. One by one they said to him, "Surely you don't mean me?"

"It is one of you," Jesus replied. "It is the one who dips bread into the bowl with me. The Son of Man will go just as it is written about him. But how terrible it will be for the one who hands over the Son of Man! It would be better for him if he had not been born."

While they were eating, Jesus took bread. He gave thanks and broke it. He handed it to his disciples and said, "Take it. This is my body."

Then he took a cup. He gave thanks and handed it to them. All of them drank from it.

"This is my blood of the covenant," he said to them. "It is poured out for many."'

SOMETHING TO THINK ABOUT

Jesus took parts of the traditional Passover meal and gave them new meaning. The Passover had celebrated freedom from slavery in Egypt. Now he used the same meal with bread and wine to show what was about to happen to him. On the cross, his body was broken; his blood poured out. Because of Jesus' death, we can be free from the consequences of our sin and rebellion against God.

The words Jesus said are used daily around the world as millions of his followers remember his death by sharing a symbolic meal together. It is known as the Lord's Supper, Holy Communion, the Mass or the Eucharist.

Jesus offers us freedom. He promises his followers a fresh start and an eternal future. The invitation is open to you today.

Prayer

Father in heaven, I'm amazed that you love me. Help me to know Jesus better. Amen.

'I want to know Christ better. Yes, I want to know the power that raised him from the dead. I want to join him in his sufferings. I want to become like him by sharing in his death. Then by God's grace I will rise from the dead.'
PHILIPPIANS 3:10-11

'Come to this table, not because you must but because you may,
not because you are strong, but because you are weak.
Come, not because any goodness of your own gives you a right to come,
but because you need mercy and help.
Come, because you love the Lord a little and would like to love him more.
Come, because he loved you and gave himself for you.
Come and meet the risen Christ, for we are his Body.'
AN INVITATION TO COMMUNION*

*From *Gathering for Worship: Patterns and Prayers for the Community of Disciples* (Norwich: Canterbury Press, 2005)

33 Abandoned

Brian's dad left home when Brian was just four. He was abused and then abandoned to a children's home. He was first caught breaking and entering as a 12-year-old and was given three years' probation. By the age of 16 Brian was living on his own and experimenting with drugs. His petty thieving led to three months in Gosport Detention Centre.

He first saw Hell's Angels during seafront riots in Brighton. They wore sleeveless denim or leather jackets and heavily studded belts. On the back of every jacket was embroidered a skull, and around it were the words 'Hell's Angels'.

'I was impressed by the way they were fighting and, when I saw that their bikes were like no other bikes I'd ever seen, it really blew my mind,' he said.

Violent temper

Brian did have a brief stint in conventional employment with the Electricity Board, but he had a violent temper. One fight too many left him jobless with only bikers, junkies and drug pushers as companions. Copying the American Hell's Angels lifestyle with a bike as his idol gave him the close-knit family he'd never had.

Drugs made his temper worse. Fights flared and finally led Brian back to prison. His first stretch in Winchester was followed by another 18-month sentence when he served time in Lewes, Wandsworth and then Chelmsford maximum-security prison.

In the autumn of 1972, Brian was back on the streets, still president of his Hell's Angels chapter, when he was arrested for the last time. He'd stabbed two skinheads in a fight in Bognor, leaving them fighting for their lives. After three months on remand in Winchester, Brian was sentenced to four years, which he was to serve in Dartmoor prison.

Rejected

Alone in his cell, he had time to think of the people he had terrorised and maimed. 'Over and over again I remembered that I had been rejected by my family. It was a scar that never healed.'

He had no visitors until the welfare officer asked if he wanted a visit to be arranged.

'OK, but I want to talk about God,' was Brian's response. When his visitor arrived and asked if there was anything he needed, Brian asked for a copy of *The Living Bible*, which he had seen advertised.

On his 27th birthday, Brian's Bible arrived together with a copy of *Run Baby Run*, about a New York gang leader called Nicky Cruz, whose life had hit rock bottom like Brian's. Nicky Cruz had asked God to change him.

Brian was in tears as he read about what God had done for Nicky. He began to read the Bible and realised that Jesus was speaking to him, offering to change his life. Brian responded out loud, inviting Jesus to make that change. He felt the love of God pour in. He woke the next morning knowing he was a new person.

Helping others

More than 40 years later, Brian's story has helped many men to make that same change. On his release, Brian lived at a Christian hostel for drug addicts for five months. He was no longer a junkie, but there he was able to see Christian love in action. Soon he began to tell his story to help others on their journey to Christ.

He attended Moorlands Bible College. The training included a two-week practical stint in London working with London City Mission, which led to a job. He now works mainly with the chaplaincy in Wandsworth prison.

'A lot of my work is with people who have failed,' Brian says, and he feels qualified to help on that score. He makes no pretence of personal success. 'I try to live with my humanity. That's the reality of following Jesus,' he adds.

Working with broken people means not every story has a happy ending, but God has given Brian genuine love for guys like him who come face-to-face with their own terrifying emptiness when the prison door bangs shut. Like Brian, many have found that Jesus helps people find lasting freedom.

You can find out more about Brian Greenaway's story in his book, *The Monster Within* (Farnham: CWR, 2012). Used with permission.

 MARK 14:32–38

'Jesus and his disciples went to a place called Gethsemane. Jesus said to them, "Sit here while I pray." He took Peter, James and John along with him. He began to be very upset

and troubled. "My soul is very sad. I feel close to death," he said to them. "Stay here. Keep watch."

He went a little farther. Then he fell to the ground. He prayed that, if possible, the hour might pass by him. "Abba, Father," he said, "everything is possible for you. Take this cup of suffering away from me. But let what you want be done, not what I want."

Then he returned to his disciples and found them sleeping. "Simon," he said to Peter, "are you asleep? Couldn't you keep watch for one hour? Watch and pray. Then you won't fall into sin when you are tempted. The spirit is willing, but the body is weak."'

SOMETHING TO THINK ABOUT

Following Jesus doesn't mean we are instantly perfect. Jesus' closest friends fell asleep when he asked them to keep watch while he prayed. We all fail, but God's amazing love covers our shortcomings.

Prayer

Dear Jesus, when I fail and let you down, thank you that you promise to forgive me. Please help me to change to be more like you. Amen.

'God, treat us kindly. You're our only hope.
First thing in the morning, be there for us!
When things go bad, help us out!'
ISAIAH 33:2, *THE MESSAGE*

34 Alone

What can I say about hope? Well, to those who suffer, who are in pain, alone, who feel the world is against them... you are not alone!

I had no father-figure growing up, and my mum was with men who beat her, drinking every day. I grew up confused and scared. I wasn't myself at school or with my friends. To make matters worse, when I was 13 I was sexually abused. Everyone was too wrapped up in their own problems, so I locked it in and depression formed. I self-harmed every day. I started to smoke cannabis. I was hurting and lashed out over and over.

'No one cares,' I kept telling myself.

Losing a daughter

I started getting into relationships with girls who were doing the same as me. They hit me. I hit them. I smoked drugs. So did they. When it went wrong, I blamed her, she blamed me.

I became a father, but then my daughter died of cot death. I was raging... burning. I hated my life and everyone who let my life get so bad. I was lashing out, head-butting walls, smashing up my flat, trying to kill myself multiple times. At home in our flat, my partner was screaming, hitting me. I lost it. I battered her – beat her up real bad. Straight after, I cried, 'Why God? Why?' I got a knife and tried to stab myself.

In prison, I couldn't handle my emotions. I screamed out to God in my cell: 'Please God, I beg you. I am so sorry for this life I have lived. I am so sick and tired of all the violence, the pain I have caused. Please! I'm willing to do it your way. I'm willing to change, to listen. Just help me. I beg you.'

At first, nothing. The next day I tried again and again. Then I felt a beautiful, light presence was on me. I could feel it around my spirit. I felt calm. I felt at peace. I was crying and crying.

God's good plans

God told me to listen and do it his way. So every day, little by little, I got to know God and his ways. He told me to let go; the past is over. I am forgiven. He is my friend. He will never leave me.

God showed me not to put my trust and hope in imperfect humans, but in himself. He told me I am loved, valued and respected. My daughter is with him in heaven and she can't wait to be reunited with her daddy when the day comes.

God told me he's got plans for me. I notice every day, when I put Jesus first, I feel this joy. My life has begun to have meaning. My actions are better. My head is clear. I am off drugs. No self-harming. No pain.

I feel free. I am dancing and singing in my cell. I am treating everybody so much better. I feel good. I am not alone. I was created to have a relationship with the true living God. I smile more. I don't have all the answers, but I know Jesus is no liar. He says, 'Seek and you will find…

You have tried it your way, now try my way. I love you so much, I want to give you joy, and to hold your hand all the way to your heavenly home, my precious, precious child. You should have all hope in the world. It's a choice. It's a way of life. It is my grace. All you have to do is make that choice. It doesn't matter how bad you feel or what you have done.'

Contributed by a prisoner.

 MARK 14:43-50

'Just as Jesus was speaking, Judas appeared. He was one of the 12 disciples. A crowd was with him. They were carrying swords and clubs. The chief priests, the teachers of the law, and the elders had sent them.

Judas, who was going to hand Jesus over, had arranged a signal with them. "The one I kiss is the man," he said. "Arrest him and have the guards lead him away." So Judas went to Jesus at once. Judas said, "Rabbi!" And he kissed Jesus. The men grabbed Jesus and arrested him. Then one of those standing nearby pulled his sword out. He struck the servant of the high priest and cut off his ear.

"Am I leading a band of armed men against you?" asked Jesus. "Do you have to come out with swords and clubs to capture me? Every day I was with you. I taught in the temple courtyard, and you didn't arrest me. But the Scriptures must come true." Then everyone left him and ran away.'

SOMETHING TO THINK ABOUT

Only a few hours before Jesus was arrested, the disciples had vowed never to leave him. But when his accusers came, the disciples all ran away. Judas had been paid 30 pieces of silver to betray Jesus (Matthew 26:15), which was the price of a slave (Exodus 21:32). Jesus was prepared to give up his life so that we can have forgiveness and a new life with him. How do you respond to his gift of new life?

Prayer

I have nothing worth giving to you, heavenly Father. You deserve everything. Thank you for giving your Son, Jesus, so I can have life. Amen.

'God so loved the world that he gave his one and only Son. Anyone who believes in him will not die but will have eternal life.'

JOHN 3:16

Week 6 – Death defeated

Since the first Easter 2,000 years ago, Christians have mourned Jesus' death and celebrated his resurrection in the days known as Holy Week. We have seen how Jesus was welcomed into Jerusalem to the shouts of 'Hosanna'. Without knowing the importance of her actions, a woman poured expensive perfume on his head, symbolically preparing his body for burial.

Jesus used bread and wine to help all his followers through history to remember his death and resurrection. He had done no wrong, but he was arrested, tried and sentenced. Crowds cried out for his execution.

He was tortured and crucified, nailed to a cross.

When he died, something deeply symbolic took place. 'The temple curtain was torn in two from top to bottom' (Mark 15:38). This was a huge curtain – too high for human hands to tear apart. It hung in front of the Holy of Holies – separating people from God's presence in the Jewish temple. When it was torn in two, it opened the way to God. That's what happened when Jesus died. Now, because of Jesus, we can all approach God.

The Roman commander who saw Jesus die would have seen many deaths. He knew that this death was different and said, 'This man was surely the Son of God!' (Mark 15:39).

But Jesus' death was not the end of the story. At the end of this six-week journey with Jesus, we celebrate his resurrection. He has risen from the dead! He lives!

READ: MARK CHAPTERS 14:53–16:20

Key verses

'The Sabbath day ended. Mary Magdalene, Mary the mother of James, and Salome bought spices. They were going to use them for Jesus' body. Very early on the first day of the week, they were on their way to the tomb. It was just after sunrise. They asked each other, "Who will roll the stone away from the entrance to the tomb?"

Then they looked up and saw that the stone had been rolled away. The stone was very large. They entered the tomb. As they did, they saw a young man dressed in a white robe. He was sitting on the right side. They were alarmed.

"Don't be alarmed," he said. "You are looking for Jesus the Nazarene, who was crucified. But he has risen! He is not here! See the place where they had put him. Go! Tell his disciples and Peter, 'He is going ahead of you into Galilee. There you will see him. It will be just as he told you.'"'
Mark 16:1-7

THINK

1. Jesus' closest friends deserted him. On the cross, Jesus felt that his own Father in heaven had deserted him too. He went through this for us, so that we never have to be alone. Can you describe times when you have been alone, but have experienced God's presence with you?

2. Our six-week journey began with Jesus' baptism and ends with Jesus talking about the importance of baptism. Have you taken this step in following Jesus?

3. Hebrews 10 explains what happened in the spiritual realm when Jesus died. It compares the Old Testament system of sacrifices with what Jesus did on the cross: 'Christ offered his body once and for all time' (Hebrews 10:10). How does this help us to understand the difference Jesus' death and resurrection has made?

4. Read Hebrews 10:22–25 and talk about how we can help each other to follow Jesus. Spend some time encouraging each other.

LIFE LESSONS

1. Baptism is a way of showing that our old life has died and a new life has begun. The prison story on Day 35 reminds us that baptism isn't about a special place or special water, but about what God does. Talk about what it means to be baptised.

2. Ani (Day 36) has found that by reading the Bible he can become friends with Jesus. Reading the Bible saved the life of the prisoner who tells his story on Day 38. What is your experience of reading the Bible?

3. Being part of a Christian church or community is an important part of following Jesus, as one ex-prisoner found (Day 39). We can help one another to become more like Jesus. How do you find the help you need to grow as a Christian?

LOOK AHEAD

Our six-week journey with Jesus from the River Jordan to Jerusalem is complete. But it is not the end of the story. Jesus wants to walk with us through the whole of our lives and he has promised he is preparing a place for us to be with him forever. Death is not the end. The best is yet to come!

35 The best is yet to come

When I first started injecting, I had a deep-seated fear that it could kill me. Towards the end of my addiction, 12 years later, the idea of it killing me had become really attractive.

It gets really dark in those smelly public toilets when you're soaked in sweat with a needle in your arm, even when it's the middle of the day. If I'd come from an abusive childhood it probably wouldn't have been so confusing, but I hadn't. I come from 'good stock'; my parents were honest, hard-working people.

When the police burst into my house in November 1989, I felt a deep sense of relief. I was glad to see them. For a split second I felt the urge to escape out of the bedroom window and across the gardens, simply because of the unbearable thought of custody without one last hit. But then I knew – if I run now, I'll have to run again tomorrow. I was arrested on suspicion of burglary and immediately admitted to it – I wanted to erase all suspicion just in case they didn't have enough evidence and I would be back on the street that same day.

Solitary

When I eventually stood before the judge at Manchester Crown Court in August 1990, I was sentenced to 30 months in prison. Within seconds I was already thinking,

'And then what? Back to my addiction?' I had not yet reached my mid-thirties and I felt that my life was as good as over.

Ten months later, I was in solitary confinement when I was told that my parole had been refused. In the solitude of that cell, I sobbed and sobbed. Everything was just dark.

With six months left to serve, I was starting to feel anxious about my release. That was the only reason I went to the chapel service – while I could see the insanity of my existence, the depth of hopelessness had become an accepted world-view for me. I assumed that I would die at the end of a syringe – and that's just the way it was.

When the pastor read from Romans 7:15–25, I realised I didn't know Jesus on a personal level. I saw the severity of being lost for eternity because my self-hatred would not let me turn to God for forgiveness.

Challenged

Then came the challenge, 'Does anyone feel the need to receive Jesus Christ as their personal Lord and Saviour?'

Within minutes I was kneeling in an improvised baptismal – an industrial waste bin full of water – being baptised. Joy just flooded my soul! Freedom engulfed me. I somehow knew I'd been 'born again'. Life was instantly seasoned by hope, significance, connection, direction, meaning and purpose. It was as instantaneous as that – I knew that Jesus had come into my life and set me free from the chains of misery and death.

I've been clean and sober now for almost 24 years. His mercies never end. I married a beautiful attorney in 2001, and in 2005 we started The Bethesda Addictions Treatment Centre. Our facility has treated men and women from all over the world since 2005 – and God's favour simply continues to astound us.

The best is yet to come.

Contributed by an ex-offender.

MARK 14:55-56,60-65

'The chief priests and the whole Sanhedrin were looking for something to use against Jesus. They wanted to put him to death. But they did not find any proof. Many witnesses lied about him. But their stories did not agree...

Then the high priest stood up in front of them. He asked Jesus, "Aren't you going to answer? What are these charges these men are bringing against you?" But Jesus remained silent. He gave no answer.

Again the high priest asked him, "Are you the Messiah? Are you the Son of the Blessed One?"

"I am," said Jesus. "And you will see the Son of Man sitting at the right hand of the Mighty One. You will see the Son of Man coming on the clouds of heaven."

The high priest tore his clothes. "Why do we need any more witnesses?" he asked...

They all found him guilty and said he must die. Then some began to spit at him. They blindfolded him. They hit him with their fists. They said, "Prophesy!" And the guards took him and beat him.'

SOMETHING TO THINK ABOUT

Jesus' trial was fixed. The religious leaders wanted Jesus dead. False witnesses had been brought in to accuse him. The charge was blasphemy – calling himself the Son of God. The scene was set for Jesus' execution.

Prayer

Father God, help me to appreciate what Jesus has done for me. Amen.

'What a terrible failure I am! Who will save me from this sin that brings death to my body? I give thanks to God who saves me. He saves me through Jesus Christ our Lord.'
ROMANS 7:24–25

'He was beaten, he was tortured,
but he didn't say a word.
Like a lamb taken to be slaughtered
and like a sheep being sheared,
he took it all in silence.'
ISAIAH 53:7–9, *THE MESSAGE*
(written 680 years before Jesus was born)

36 Denial and discovery

Igor is discovering Christianity for the first time through Bible studies at Heathrow's Immigration Removal Centre.

He arrived in the UK 'to visit a friend' ten years ago. He came from his home in Uzbekistan 'without any documents', and now refuses to return because he does not recognise the political status of his home country.

'I'm not a citizen of Uzbekistan,' he says, 'I was born in the Soviet Union.' So, it's perhaps not a surprise that he finds himself at the Heathrow Immigration Removal Centre awaiting deportation.

It's here that he is discovering Christianity for the first time, taking part in a weekly Bible study led by Russian chaplain, Dmitri Sorokin.

Soviet citizen

'In the Soviet Union, religion was nothing,' Igor says. 'I didn't get into the Bible there. I came into it since arriving at the detention centre. I don't have a Bible of my own,' he adds, 'but I'd like to because then I could read it in my own room.'

Igor has spent ten years working in IT in Britain, but as part of the black economy. 'I work in IT, so work is not a problem,' he says. 'I have friends here. But without documents I can't travel. I am stuck.' He looks resigned to being deported. 'I'm too old to start again,' he says.

Studying the Bible is proving to be a very positive

distraction in a time of uncertainty. 'I've just started to read the Bible,' he says. 'We're studying John. It's interesting for me now.'

Uncertainty

Ani is also in Heathrow's Immigration Removal Centre. He lives in constant uncertainty about his future. He believes only God can sustain him. He shakes constantly as he talks, tapping his feet and his hands. 'It's just a miracle that I'm still here,' he says.

Ani's story started like so many others, full of hope. He came to the UK in 2013 with a place to study Chemical Engineering at the University of Swansea.

'Things got messy,' he says, without expanding on what that means. But whatever it involved, that messiness meant that Ani had to re-sit a year. That pushed him over his three-year visa and he was brought to the Immigration Removal Centre. 'I hope that I will be sent back to Swansea to finish my studies,' he says. But given his brush with deportation, it seems unlikely.

Closer to God

Ani comes from a Christian background and received a Bible from one of the chaplains at the centre.

'I feel closer to God than I did before,' says Ani, 'because, you know, when you are "out" [living outside the detention centre in society] you are working; there's always something going on. But here, there's the whole time, so I can just read and make friends with this guy,' he says, pointing to his Bible.

'This place is enough to drive you crazy,' he says. 'You are scared. You don't know what's going to happen the next minute, or hour, let alone tomorrow. You are living in uncertainty. I just believe that it's only God who can sustain me and get me out of this.'

Contributed by Bible Society. Used with permission.

 MARK 14:66-72

'Peter was below in the courtyard. One of the high priest's female servants came by. When she saw Peter warming himself, she looked closely at him.

"You also were with Jesus, that Nazarene," she said.

But Peter said he had not been with him. "I don't know or understand what you're talking about," he said. He went out to the entrance to the courtyard.

The servant saw him there. She said again to those standing around, "This fellow is one of them." Again he said he was not.

After a little while, those standing nearby said to Peter, "You must be one of them. You are from Galilee."

Then Peter began to curse. He said to them, "I don't know this man you're talking about!"

Right away the rooster crowed the second time. Then Peter remembered what Jesus had spoken to him. "The rooster will crow twice," he had said. "Before it does, you will say three times that you don't know me." Peter broke down and cried.'

SOMETHING TO THINK ABOUT

Peter failed Jesus – he denied that he even knew him. But after Jesus rose from the dead, he forgave Peter and recommissioned him. When Jesus ascended into heaven, Peter was among the disciples when they received the gift of God's Holy Spirit. He became a powerful preacher, boldly declaring to the crowd in Jerusalem: 'All of you must turn away from your sins and be baptized in the name of Jesus Christ. Then your sins will be forgiven. You will receive the gift of the Holy Spirit' (Acts 2:38).

Prayer

Forgive me, Jesus, when I block you out of parts of my life. Help me to follow you wholeheartedly. Amen.

'Don't worry about anything. No matter what happens, tell God about everything. Ask and pray, and give thanks to him. Then God's peace will watch over your hearts and your minds. He will do this because you belong to Christ Jesus. God's peace can never be completely understood.'
PHILIPPIANS 4:6–7

'God did not send his Son into the world to judge the world. He sent his Son to save the world through him.'
JOHN 3:17

37 Rock bottom

Born in Berwick Hills, Middlesbrough, Gram enjoyed a happy, close-knit, working class childhood – but he was soon getting into mischief. At nine years old he went into the pub near his home and, on a pretext, got the barmaid to go out the back. He nipped through the serving hatch, grabbed a big bag of crisps and dashed out. But the bag wasn't full of crisps. It was a cash-bag with £50 inside. So he went straight to the nearest sweet shop to splash out. But the owner saw the bag and informed the landlord. Gram was caught red-handed.

Childish high spirits? Perhaps, but theft became a way of life for Gram, and at 16 he was given his first sentence – four months for breaking and entering. He wasn't much good at school, so he'd soon realised that it was easier for him to let his fists do the talking.

Football hooligan

In the 1980s, a lad with a penchant for violence was easily drawn to the mayhem being caused at football grounds around the country. Gram joined a hooligan gang that followed Middlesbrough Football Club. He travelled all over the country with them – when he wasn't doing time.

Fight followed fight. Injury followed injury: his right eye was slashed; a bottle in his face nearly cost him his left eye; he was hit over the head with a blunt sword; a craft knife slashed his chin; he was bitten by a police dog;

he was stabbed four times; the end of his little finger was chopped off...

Between 1980 and 1990, Gram was jailed a further four times for football related violence, assault, robbery and theft. He returned to Teesside at Christmas 1992 and began to drink heavily. Cannabis followed, then heroin and crack cocaine.

Hospitalised

In 1993, he attempted to take his own life by slashing his wrists. But a patrolling police car found him in the early hours of the morning, and he was saved in hospital.

Home for Gram was a bench outside the Post Office on Grange Road in Middlesbrough. Food was begged or scavenged. Sleeping outside in all weathers, he would wake up in winter with his shirt stiff with ice from rain, and his jeans stiff from where he'd soiled himself. Even so, when a passing group of Christian evangelists called out, 'Jesus loves you', he found the strength to chase them.

Finally, in August 1996, his body gave out and he went into a coma. He was taken to hospital with a litany of complaints: septicemia, malnourishment, hypothermia, liver damage, kidney failure.

The coma lasted six days, during which time his mother was advised to prepare to have the life-support machine switched off. Every day, the same group of Christians who Gram had chased came to the hospital to pray for him.

Rescued

He was in hospital for two months. He had lost his sight, and after seven weeks had to be taught how to walk again. However, he knew something had changed. He went on his first Alpha course at the Oakwood Centre on Teesside. A slow healing had started. (He has now led more than 100 of these courses himself.)

In November 1996, Gram welcomed Jesus into his life and sat weeping with joy. He married Natasha in June 1999, and they now have two sons. They live in the Stockton area, where Gram now helps young offenders and other prisoners find God's amazing love and forgiveness, just like he did.

Read Gram Seed's story in his book, *One Step Beyond: One Man's Journey from Near Death to New Life* (Farnham: CWR, 2008). Used with permission.

MARK 15:1,6–15

'*So they tied Jesus up and led him away. Then they handed him over to Pilate... It was the usual practice at the Passover Feast to let one prisoner go free. The people could choose the one they wanted. A man named Barabbas was in prison. He was there with some other people who had fought against the country's rulers. They had committed murder...*

"Do you want me to let the king of the Jews go free?" asked Pilate... But the chief priests stirred up the crowd. So the crowd asked Pilate to let Barabbas go free instead.

"Then what should I do with the one you call the king of the Jews?" Pilate asked them.

"Crucify him!" the crowd shouted.

"Why? What wrong has he done?" asked Pilate.

But they shouted even louder, "Crucify him!"

Pilate wanted to satisfy the crowd. So he let Barabbas go free. He ordered that Jesus be whipped. Then he handed him over to be nailed to a cross.'

SOMETHING TO THINK ABOUT

Jesus, who had never done anything wrong, took the place of a murderer on death row. He chooses to take our place, too, when we sin. As Paul explained to the Romans, 'Everyone has sinned. No one measures up to God's glory. The free gift of God's grace makes us right with him. Christ Jesus paid the price to set us free' (Romans 3:23–24).

Prayer

Jesus, I can't thank you enough for what you have done for me. Thank you. Amen.

'When you sin, the pay you get is death. But God gives you the gift of eternal life. That's because of what Christ Jesus our Lord has done.'

ROMANS 6:23

38 He died for you

In August 2006, I'd made the decision I had wanted to make for over three years. I was going to take my own life. I'd lost the will to live.

I was serving a life sentence for murder, the result of me 'losing it' during a drunken argument. I couldn't remember what had happened, which only compounded the dreadful remorse I felt on a daily basis.

It was 8.45pm, and I was in a cell in the segregation unit known to inmates as 'The Chokey'. At around 9pm, the day shift would hand over to their night time colleagues. It would be then that I would hang myself. Just 15 minutes to wait – no more pain, no more shame. Relief from the awful situation I was in.

Inner voice

But I was interrupted. It was as if a quiet voice spoke to me: 'Just read that Bible'. On the shelf was a Gideon New Testament and Psalms. Until then, it had been just a blue object in my cell. My mind answered immediately, 'What good is that going to do me?' Again the voice replied, 'Just read that Bible.' Again, my mind retaliated with, 'What's the point?'

But the inner quiet voice persisted: 'Just read that Bible.' I remember thinking that it would pass the time until the night shift took over.

I opened the book at the beginning. It was a list of names – nothing inspirational there. I read on: 'So and so, the son of so and so' and so forth. Blah, blah, blah! But something was stirring inside me. I stumbled across a particular verse on the page: 'and Jacob the father of Joseph, the husband of Mary, of whom was born Jesus, who is called Christ'.

Tears

A massive realisation came over me. I remember exclaiming, 'Wow, he is real!' From then on I could not stop reading through the Gospel. I shed tears as I read the Beatitudes, but I still had no hope. Surely God couldn't accept me. I was past being forgiven.

I tried to put the book down, but could not. Something was urging me on. Then, at Luke 15:11–32, I found the parable of the lost son (see page 116). As I read, the tears started again – but with a difference. The hopelessness that had been always constant, disappeared. The wretchedness I suffered also went. Most of all, the idea I firmly believed that I was unworthy of forgiveness was taken from me.

The angry, frightened, desperate person I had become ceased to exist there and then. At verse 32, when Jesus' words spoke of the brother who was 'dead and is alive again; he was lost and is found', I was found indeed. I wept openly with joy. Suddenly, I had hope. I couldn't have told you what for, I just knew I had hope. I wanted to live; there wasn't any difficulty I wasn't ready to face. My words can't do justice to what was happening in and around me.

Alive!

I spent the rest of the evening reading Scripture. I was alive! I could pray! I was no longer alone. I was talking with Jesus. I couldn't see him, but he was there.

A few days later I was taken from the segregation unit and returned to one of the wings. I asked to see the chaplain. He was a bit wary of me, as some weeks previously I'd been a bit unpleasant. I told him what had happened. He asked if I would be going to chapel on Sunday, and I said yes. That Sunday, I went to the front and gave my life to Jesus at the altar.

Almost three years later, my life as a Christian is unrecognisable from the lost soul I was in that segregation cell. Not only has God transformed me, he has given me gifts; blessings that would fill a book. A life full of hope, love and peace. I am no longer useless but useful. Today I owe my life to Jesus – I know he gently spoke to me that night. Without him I have nothing; I am nothing.

In all of this, the Gideons supplied the Bible. Thank you, Gideons – your work in prisons makes such a difference. I'm proof.

Contributed by Gideons International. Used with permission.

MARK 15:25-32

'It was nine o'clock in the morning when they crucified him. They wrote out the charge against him. It read,

    THE KING OF THE JEWS.

    They crucified with him two rebels against Rome.

One was on his right and one was on his left. Those who passed by shouted at Jesus and made fun of him. They shook their heads and said, "So you are going to destroy the temple and build it again in three days? Then come down from the cross! Save yourself!" In the same way the chief priests and the teachers of the law made fun of him among themselves. "He saved others," they said. "But he can't save himself! Let this Messiah, this king of Israel, come down now from the cross! When we see that, we will believe." Those who were being crucified with Jesus also made fun of him.'

SOMETHING TO THINK ABOUT

Jesus hadn't committed any crime. He was not found guilty. The men crucified with him were being punished for the crimes they had committed. Luke, another of the Gospel writers, described how one of the men had a change of heart. He said, 'We are getting just what our actions call for. But this man hasn't done anything wrong.' Then he said, 'Jesus, remember me when you come into your kingdom' (Luke 23:41–42).

Prayer

Thank you, Jesus, for dying so I can be forgiven and live with you forever. Amen.

'He is no fool who gives what he cannot keep to gain what he cannot lose.'
JIM ELLIOT (1927–1857)

39 It's not over yet

A fair way into my 11-year prison sentence, I sat in my cell, doing a lot of reading and thinking. I felt I needed to understand myself and why I had done bad things, and I began to write a journal about my life.

Out of the blue, I began writing about the things I'd heard about Jesus before I went to prison. My mum said she could hear angels (I thought she was off her head), and my sister was very aware of Jesus. I thought of some of my teachers at school; they were Christians who had made such a positive impact on my early years.

I was brought up in Willesden in London. We were a poor family but we survived, although often I couldn't have what other kids had and that made me jealous. As a young lad I got into quite a lot of fights, heavy drinking and taking drugs. I was violent, and when the police came to arrest me, they came in force. They knew I wouldn't come quietly. I had robbed a few banks and ended up with the 11-year sentence. I had a sense of guilt – not because I'd robbed banks, but because I felt like I'd hurt a lot of people.

Angels?

One day, I was reading a book that quoted some Bible verses. I wanted to read the Bible to check out what was said, so I went to the prison chaplain. 'Can I have a Bible?' I asked. Just at that moment, a crowd of inmates surrounded me and one of them handed me a Bible.

'I'll give it back,' I said, but when I went back to look for the guy who had given me the Bible, I couldn't find him anywhere. I asked one of the prison officers if someone had just been discharged. No one had been discharged for three days. I never saw the guy again. I wonder if he was an angel.

I went along to the chaplaincy, and a guy was talking about some murders that had taken place in Northern Ireland. He also spoke of how Jesus died for the sins of the world. I went back to my cell, amazed at what I had heard. I wondered if I could really be forgiven.

My life changed massively. I knew, I believed: Jesus was the answer to everything. I read the Bible. I found it really spoke to me – and it still does.

I completed my prison sentence and began visiting some churches. There were lots of 'hellos', but not much else. People were unwilling to get to know me. I carried the stigma of prison. I became a nomad Christian.

Community

One day I was sitting in my flat, thinking of all the people I knew in prison. I started hitchhiking around the country, looking for them. I came to Northampton hoping to find my friend, Pete. I knew his sister. She had visited me in prison when I had no other visitors. I went to the house where she lives, a Christian community house in Northampton. The leader said, 'Come and spend a weekend with us.' I've been there ever since.

I like my space, and community life is not always easy for me. But a while back I sensed God say, 'I thought you wanted to know my love. I'll teach it through every one of these people you share the house with.'

The guys are very down-to-earth. We're not afraid to tell each other about what's going on in our hearts – the good and the bad. That's the way we get healed. In community, we're all in it together. I find that when something's really getting to me, the answer often comes from someone else. God speaks to us through each other.

How far will we let God go to get our attention? He got my attention in prison, but my testimony never stops. Sometimes I think of the Roman soldiers throwing a dice for Jesus' clothes as Jesus looked down on them from the cross. We can be like that – throwing the dice for the bits of Jesus we want. But he is massive, and I want to embrace all of him.

Contributed by www.christiancommunity.org.uk and used with permission.

 MARK 15:33–39

'At noon, darkness covered the whole land. It lasted three hours. At three o'clock in the afternoon Jesus cried out in a loud voice, "Eloi, Eloi, lema sabachthani?" This means "My God, my God, why have you deserted me?"

Some of those standing nearby heard Jesus cry out. They said, "Listen! He's calling for Elijah."...

With a loud cry, Jesus took his last breath.

The temple curtain was torn in two from top to bottom. A Roman commander was standing there in front of Jesus. He saw how Jesus died. Then he said, "This man was surely the Son of God!"'

SOMETHING TO THINK ABOUT

In the temple in Jerusalem, a heavy curtain symbolically separated the people from the most holy place. The priest entered just once a year, after making a special sacrifice to gain forgiveness for the people. As Hebrews 9:12 explains: 'He [Jesus] entered the Most Holy Room by spilling his own blood. He did it once and for all time. In this way, he paid the price to set us free from sin forever.'

Prayer

Dear Father God, thank you that because Jesus was separated from you on the cross, I can be free from the consequences of my own shortcomings. I can approach you as your adopted, much-loved child. Help me to respond to your love. Amen.

'My God, my God, why have you deserted me? Why do you seem so far away when I need you to save me?'
PSALM 22:1 (written by David 1,000 years before Jesus lived)

'Jesus gave one sacrifice for the sins of the people. He gave it once and for all time. He did it by offering himself.'
HEBREWS 7:27

40 Jesus is alive!

Ben* spent some sleepless nights in prison going 'cold turkey'. There were no books, no clock, no television... just the bare bricks to count and his cellmate's snoring to listen to.

'I knew after such an awful first night – and with the prospect of more to follow – I had to do something,' Ben says. So he asked for a Bible.

Ben had been part of a church youth club in Leicester when growing up, but had stopped going to church at 16. Petty crime and joyriding led to a stint in a detention centre. When he got out, he got a job as a waiter and started smoking cannabis.

'When I was 19 I moved to Brighton. I was experimenting with drugs. I thought I was having a good time, enjoying myself and would come to no harm. Then I came back to Leicestershire. My flatmate was a heroin addict, so I started experimenting with that too. I was also a cannabis dealer. I was arrested and sentenced to 18 months in prison.'

Addicted

When Ben got out, he managed to find work. But his occasional drug use developed to heroin dependency. 'Without it I could not get out of bed,' Ben says. 'I was often late for work, so I lost my job.' He joined other addicts and resorted to petty crime to fund his addiction. 'In September 2003 I was sentenced to one month in prison for shoplifting in breach of probation.'

Ben knew he was facing 'cold turkey' – with no access to heroin, addicts have overwhelming cravings for the drug, along with sweating, chills, nausea, vomiting, abdominal cramps and diarrhoea. With only a Bible to distract him from the agonies he was going through, he flicked to the story of Job.

'I was thinking it was pretty irrelevant, but then I read that Job too had had no sleep for seven days and nights because of his sores and various afflictions. Unlike me, he didn't deserve to suffer,' Ben says.

Yelling at God

'By the seventh night I was at my wits end, going crazy with the pain. I got cross with God. "This is your book," I yelled at him. "You're my 'heavenly Father'. My earthly father loves me and he would do all he could to help make me sleep. I am asking you for some sleep." No apparent response. I resumed pleading, but this time I thought I would be more polite: "If you give me some sleep, I will give you my life." I heard a voice in my head: "Never mind what you want. What about what I want of you?" I carried on ranting and raving. Still nothing. Eventually I said, "OK, tell me what you want."'

Ben felt directed to a specific verse in an Old Testament book written by the prophet Joel: 'Wake up, you drunkards, and weep!' (Joel 1:5, NIV).

'The words hit me. I knew it was God. The drunkard was me on drugs, and the weeping was about my need to repent. It all applied to me. I was gobsmacked. I kept saying to myself, "God the creator is communicating with me." I knew I was waking up spiritually. I told him, "I believe. I know this is your Word. I know Jesus is your Son, that he is the way of salvation. I know I have upset my family, and more importantly you. Help! I need to come back to you."'

Floods of tears

Ben started praying for his family and the weeping started. 'I was in floods of tears. "I'm sorry" was all I could say for about 15 minutes. It was from my soul, from my heart. It was repentance. Then I felt something, as if a touch, and I had total peace.'

Ben started singing a song he'd heard years before, then found himself worshipping God and making a promise: 'Every moment of my life is yours. Every day I will seek to give myself to you.' Then he fell asleep for three or four hours.

Looking back, Ben says, 'So many try the religious bit while in prison, but I was genuine. I came out in October 2003 and joined the local church.'

He got baptised, and by early January he had a job at a conference centre as a waiter. Now he is married with three children. He's a dustbin lorry driver and the family play an active part in the local church.

'I used to think taking drugs was exciting, but now I wake up excited each day and talk with the creator of the universe. I am not perfect. I still slip up, but I know God uses me every day.'

*Names have been changed. Contributed by an ex-offender.

MARK 16:1-7

'Mary Magdalene, Mary the mother of James, and Salome bought spices. They were going to use them for Jesus' body. Very early on the first day of the week, they were on their way to the tomb. It was just after sunrise. They asked each other, "Who will roll the stone away from the entrance to the tomb?"

Then they looked up and saw that the stone had been rolled away. The stone was very large. They entered the tomb. As they did, they saw a young man dressed in a white robe. He was sitting on the right side. They were alarmed.

"Don't be alarmed," he said. "You are looking for Jesus the Nazarene, who was crucified. But he has risen!"'

SOMETHING TO THINK ABOUT

The world changed forever on the weekend that Jesus died and rose again. The same power that raised Jesus from the dead is available to us today. Millions of people through history, around the globe, have discovered that Jesus is alive! He invites us to be part of his family.

Prayer

Thank you, Jesus, for facing the cross because you love me. I'm sorry for all my shortcomings. Please change me and help me to draw on your power for living. Help me to love the people I meet, as you love me. Amen.

CONTACTS

CARING FOR EX-OFFENDERS
www.caringforexoffenders.org
Caring for Ex-Offenders
Holy Trinity Brompton
Brompton Road
London
SW7 1JA

COMMUNITY CHAPLAINCY ASSOCIATION
www.communitychaplaincy.org.uk
Community Chaplaincy Association
C/O Peninsula Initiative Community Chaplaincy
Wat Tyler House
King William Street
Exeter
EX4 6PD

HOPE
www.hopetogether.org.uk
HOPE
8A Market Place
Rugby
CV21 3DU

JESUS HOUSE
www.jesushouse.org.uk
Jesus House for all the nations
112 Brent Terrace
Brent Cross
London
NW2 1LT

PRISON FELLOWSHIP

www.prisonfellowship.org.uk
Prison Fellowship England and Wales
PO Box 68226
London
SW1P 9WR

REFLEX

www.reflex.org
Reflex
Unit D2, Business Park East
Coombswood Way
Halesowen
West Midlands
B62 8BH

THE SALVATION ARMY

www.salvationarmy.org.uk
The Salvation Army UK and Republic of Ireland
Territorial Headquarters
101 Newington Causeway
London
SE1 6BN

THE WELCOME DIRECTORY

www.welcomedirectory.org.uk
The Welcome Directory
27 Tavistock Square
London
WC1H 9HH

NOTES

NOTES

NOTES

NOTES

||||| || PRISONS WEEK
A WEEK OF PRAYER

Prisons Week equips and enables the Church to pray for all those affected by prisons: prisoners and their families, victims of crime and their communities, those working in the criminal justice system and the many people who are involved in caring for those affected by crime on the inside and outside of our prisons. Prisons Week produces resources and provides an annual focus and reason for Christians to unite together in prayer that moves the heart of God to action.

Prisons Sunday – the second Sunday in October – marks the beginning of the week of prayer each year, running through until the following Saturday.

For more information visit **prisonsweek.org**

Waverley Abbey Resources currently donates Bible reading notes and products to prisons in the UK and overseas. To donate to Waverley Abbey Resources visit **waverleyabbeyresources.org/make-a-donation**

e are a charity serving Christians around the world with actical resources and teaching. We support you to grow your Christian faith, understand the times in which we e, and serve God in every sphere of life.

waverleyabbeycollege.ac.uk

waverleyabbeyresources.org

waverleyabbeyhouse.org